The Complete **FILMS** *of*

ERROL FLYNN

The Complete FILMS *of*

ERROL FLYNN

A Citadel Press Book
Published by Carol Publishing Group

Tony Rudy Clifford
Thomas Behlmer McCarty

Foreword by

GREER GARSON

First Carol Publishing Group Edition 1990

Copyright © 1969 by Tony Thomas,
Rudy Behlmer and Clifford McCarthy

A Citadel Press Book
Published by Carol Publishing Group

Editorial Offices	Sales & Distribution Offices
600 Madison Avenue	120 Enterprise Avenue
New York, NY 10022	Secaucus, NJ 07094

In Canada: Musson Book Company
A division of General Publishing Co. Limited
Don Mills, Ontario

Citadel Press is a registered trademark of
Carol Communications, Inc.

Queries regarding rights and permissions
should be addressed to: Carol Publishing Group,
600 Madison Avenue, New York, NY 10022

Designed by William Meinhardt

Manufactured in the United States of America
ISBN 0-8065-0237-1

20 19 18 17 16 15 14 13 12 11 10

Carol Publishing Group books are available at special discounts
for bulk purchases, for sales promotions, fund raising, or
educational purposes. Special editions can also be created to
specifications. For details contact: Special Sales Department,
Carol Publishing Group, 120 Enterprise Ave., Secaucus, NJ 07094

**The excerpt from *My First Hundred Years in Hollywood*
by Jack L. Warner is used with the permission of its
publisher, Random House, Inc., New York. Copyright 1964, 1965.**

Contents

Foreword   7

PART 1 • THE EVOLUTION OF A CAVALIER   11
In the Wake of the Bounty   21
Murder at Monte Carlo   23
The Case of the Curious Bride   26
Don't Bet on Blondes   28
Captain Blood   30

PART 2 • THE PINNACLE ERA   33
The Charge of the Light Brigade   44
Green Light   51
The Prince and the Pauper   53
Another Dawn   54
The Perfect Specimen   58
The Adventures of Robin Hood   60
Four's a Crowd   68
The Sisters   70
The Dawn Patrol   73
Dodge City   77
The Private Lives of Elizabeth and Essex   82
Virginia City   87
The Sea Hawk   91
Santa Fe Trail   97
Footsteps in the Dark   101
Dive Bomber   103
They Died With Their Boots On   106
Desperate Journey   112
Gentleman Jim   115

PART 3 • THE SLOW DEFLATION 119
Edge of Darkness 126
Thank Your Lucky Stars 130
Northern Pursuit 132
Uncertain Glory 134
Objective Burma 137
San Antonio 141
Never Say Goodbye 144
Cry Wolf 146
Escape Me Never 148
Silver River 151
Adventures of Don Juan 154
It's a Great Feeling 160
That Forsyte Woman 161
Montana 165
Rocky Mountain 167
Kim 170
Hello God 173
Adventures of Captain Fabian 174
Mara Maru 176
Against All Flags 178
Cruise of the Zaca 181
Deep Sea Fishing 183

PART 4 • THE LAST SEVEN YEARS 185
The Master of Ballantrae 192
Crossed Swords 195
William Tell 197
Let's Make Up 199
The Warriors 202
King's Rhapsody 205
Istanbul 207
The Big Boodle 209
The Sun Also Rises 211
Too Much, Too Soon 214
The Roots of Heaven 217
Cuban Rebel Girls 220

Miss Garson and Flynn in That Forsyte Woman

Foreword

by GREER GARSON

Dear Reader—Surprised to find Mrs. Miniver between the covers with Don Juan and Robin Hood?

So am I.

Usually the foreword to a book is written by an authority on either the subject or the author. I cannot qualify on either count. The honour fell to me mainly, I suspect, because my screen image contrasts piquantly with that of Errol Flynn.

But please accept a brief word, anyhow, from one who has found this book most interesting reading. I think you will enjoy it, too, as a definitive record of a film star's unique career, and a correlated and perceptive portrait of the real-life personality as it differed from or duplicated his alter ego on the screen.

The paradox of the actor is always an intriguing study. Those in the audience who stop to think about it at all must wonder how often is the laughing Pagliacci hiding a broken heart? And is it possible that our swash-buckling screen hero in real life is an insecure, lonely and unhappy man...?

Personally, I believe the contrast is seldom that absolute. Actors, like other people, are not usually sharply schizophrenic so much as a complex of overlapping and interrelated qualities, both active and latent. Consider this book for example...it could well have been titled "The Mask and the Man," for while Errol Flynn will be remembered by movie fans as the handsome, confident cavalier, the romantic conqueror in boudoir and battlefield, his friends and companions also will remember facets totally at variance with the heroic illusion. But they will remember, too, his wit and charm, his life-long love of ocean and sailing ships, his fascination with sagas of buccaneers and soldiers of fortune, and his desire to live life fully as a gay, daring adventure—and these were characteristics which reconciled the man and the image.

Surely no actor could impersonate so splendidly Robin Hood, Don Juan, Captain Blood and the rest, unless he had some of their potential within himself. Unfortunately, he had little satisfaction in playing these roles and felt frustrated by continually being typecast. What a pity he couldn't thoroughly enjoy playing the dashing hero, knowing that he was nonpareil in this field, and that he was able to make a unique contribution by bringing into our careful, regimented world a bright flash of poetry-in-action and deeds of derring-do.

The reminiscences collected from many people for this book are revealing and, interestingly enough, quite consistent; maybe, after all, we are pretty good at seeing through each other's disguises! I remember my own impression when I met Errol Flynn for the first time, except for casual encounters at social and industry events, when we were co-starred in *That Forsyte Woman* at MGM. We greeted each other warily on the first day of shooting, in an electric atmosphere of mutual apprehension, while gleeful columnists and set-siders waited breathlessly for the predicted clash between MGM's Nice Lady and Warners' Bad Boy. It never came. Instead, there was swift rapport, easy friendship, and a deal of harmless fun and laughter . . . happy memories of a picture that wasn't much, I am afraid, for the audience, but was a ball for the cast and crew that made it.

I found Errol much more objective and modest than many performers. He was satirically deprecating about himself as a screen idol and as the target of scandal journalists and night-club comedians. In our picture he tackled a new type of role and revealed an unsuspected and admirable talent for characterization. "Thank Heaven—at last an escape from cloak and dagger stuff!" he remarked. If he had lived longer—and more temperately—he would probably have emerged as the serious actor he longed to be, although I think eventually he would have preferred to earn a reputation as a writer. Another irony: the celebrated Casanova was no doubt a great man with the ladies (although I am sure he never bothered any woman who didn't *want* to be bothered), but he probably preferred the company of men and fellow roisterers. I think women baffled him. He was going through the breakup of his second marriage at the time the picture was being filmed, and he was deeply disturbed about it. He never discussed his personal problems, but any passing references to his ex-wives and his children were always courteous, humorous but without malice, and with an unmistakable underlying feeling of affection and rueful regret.

Soon afterwards, he left for England, hoping to unwind and relax by putting some distance between himself and his then current difficulties. He was facing a blue phase of personal loneliness and professional uncertainty, and he knew it, but he took leave of us all with his customary debonair insouciance. I met him a few years later at a friend's party in New York, and for one startled moment I didn't recognize him, he looked so ill and changed.

His life was one of highs and lows, and he burned himself out much too soon. In thinking of him, let us remember, above all, that to millions of people the world over he brought exhilarating and joyous entertainment, and lifted their imagination and their spirits out of the doldrums and tensions of day-to-day living with a glorious vision of adventure, chivalry and romance.

Acknowledgments

For their generous cooperation, the authors wish to thank the following individuals and organizations: Mildred Simpson and staff, Library of the Academy of Motion Picture Arts and Sciences; Nora Eddington Black; Henry Blanke; Myron Braum; Joseph Brenner; The British Film Institute; Lori C. Browne; Meredith Brucker, MGM Documentary Dept.; Jack Cardiff; Albert Cavens; Howard Christie; John Cocchi; Earl Conrad; Delmer Daves; George Eastman House; Gabe Essoe; Robert Florey; Weimar Gard; Joy Genese; Carl Hibler; Frank Larkin; Bill Latham, Warner Bros.-Seven Arts; John Lebold; Bob Lee; Mort Lickter, Warner Bros.-Seven Arts; George Lugg, Australian Council of Film Societies; Joseph R. Mass; Seton I. Miller; Hal Mohr; The Museum of Modern Art; National Telefilm Associates; Gunnard Nelson; George C. Pratt; Frank Rodriguez, Twentieth Century-Fox; Carl Schaefer, Warner Bros.-Seven Arts; Vincent Sherman; Sherry Shourds; United Artists; Universal Pictures; B. C. Van Hecke; George Vieira; Raoul Walsh; Rosemary Flynn Warner; Warner Bros.-Seven Arts; Stephen Ziskin.

Part One

The Evolution
of a Cavalier

With Olivia de Havilland in They Died With Their Boots On

Flynn at the age of four

"HE was one of the wild characters of the world," said Ann Sheridan, who appeared in three films and one teleplay with Errol Flynn, "but he also had a strange, quiet side. He camouflaged himself completely. In all the years I knew him, I never knew what really lay underneath, and I doubt if many people did."

When Flynn died, newspaper editors quickly sought opinions from people who had worked with him, particularly the actresses. Olivia de Havilland was the actress whose assessment they wanted most. She had co-starred with Flynn in eight films, six of them among his most successful vehicles. They were a perfect screen couple, but most of their films were action, costume pictures, and appearing in them was one of the reasons Olivia rebelled against Warner Brothers.

Years later in Paris, Olivia de Havilland went to see *The Adventures of Robin Hood* and realized, belatedly, what a fine film it is. Seeing the picture brought back memories and she wrote Flynn a long letter. "An apology twenty years late," she says. "But I tore it up. I reconsidered, deciding Errol would think I was silly. I'll always be sorry. A few months later he was dead. Seeing *Robin Hood* after all these years made me realize how good all our adventure films were, and I wrote Errol that I was glad I had been in every scene of them."

Olivia remembers Flynn with the kind of sad regret mixed with amusement and affection felt by those who were close to him. "He was a charming and magnetic man, but so tormented. I don't know about what, but tormented. I had a crush on him, and later I found he did for me. In fact, he proposed, but he was not divorced from Lili Damita so it was just as well that I had said no. A couple of years before he died I had an unhappy experience in Hollywood. A tall man kissed me on the back of the neck at a party and I whirled around in anger and said, 'Do I know you?' Then I realized it was Errol. He had changed so. His eyes were so sad. I had stared into them in enough movies to know his spirit was gone. It was so tragic—his death. I'm so sorry I didn't mail that letter."

To anyone who knew Flynn at all well it came as a shock but no surprise that he died at the age of fifty. The surprise was that he lasted that long. Flynn lived behind his façade of rollicking gaiety so well that few knew him to be a man with fears and depressions and feelings of self-disgust. Seemingly extroverted and hedonistic, Flynn was also introspective. With a cavalier flourish he would say, "I allow myself to be known as a colorful fragment in a drab world," but in his later years he would often sit and wonder why he had wasted so much of himself.

Errol Flynn was an amusing man. No one could make more humorous aphorisms about Flynn than he himself. Typical was: "My problem lies in reconciling my gross habits with my net income." He believed the public was entitled to a "good show," as he put it, and he was more than willing to perpetuate the image of himself as Rabelaisian and roguish. But Flynn resented any invasion of his privacy, and for the most part journalists found him to be a difficult and unco-operative subject for interviewing. He was in many ways a deceptive man. It was not until the publication of his autobiography *My Wicked, Wicked Ways*—ironically posthumous—that the inner Flynn was revealed.

Errol Flynn was born in one seaport of the British Commonwealth—Hobart, Tasmania, on June 20, 1909—and died in another—Vancouver, B.C., on October 14, 1959. Despite his Irish name and monumental gift for blarney, Flynn's parents were Australians. His mother, Marelle Young, was a daughter of a sea captain. His father, Professor Theodore Thomson Flynn, was a distinguished marine biologist and zoologist. The professor was a member of the faculty of the University of Tasmania and was also the Royal Commissioner of Tasmanian Fisheries. In 1931 he was appointed as a professor of biology to Queen's University, Belfast, Northern Ireland, which post he held until 1948. His work brought him many citations, including the MBE (Member of the British Empire). Errol Flynn described the one true love of his life as being the ocean, and this he came by honestly.

Flynn spent half of his fifty years as a film actor and appeared in some sixty films. Eight of those films are among the best of their kind, and they assure him a place in the annals of film-making: *The Charge of the Light Brigade, The Adventures of Robin Hood, The Dawn Patrol, The Sea Hawk, They Died with Their Boots On, Gentleman Jim, Objective, Burma!* and *Adventures of Don Juan.*

A film actor is remembered for his image, and the image of Errol Flynn that survives is that of the supreme swashbuckler, boldly heroic and dashing. He did it with a grace and style that was almost poetic. At first he thought it was fun, but

Flynn as a sixteen-year-old schoolboy. On the back of this he wrote: "To the best father in the world, from one of the worst sons, Errol."

over the years he grew tired of the role and longed to get away from it. It wasn't until the end of his life that he played something completely different; in three of his last films—*The Sun Also Rises, Too Much, Too Soon,* and *The Roots of Heaven*—he played alcoholics. Yet this too was a form of type-casting. Always a heavy drinker, by then his system was sodden with alcohol.

For all his failings and frustrations, Errol Flynn lived a full and flavorsome life; his fifty years were overstuffed with adventures, some real and many ridiculous, a lot of them hilarious and a few tragic. But the qualities that made him a rebel and a roisterer in life combined to make him a great and natural film star. The face, the figure, the façade, the flair were perfection for a celluloid hero.

It was as an adventurer that Flynn was presented in many of his films and no actor ever came to the craft better prepared. Before his success in Hollywood Flynn was an adventurer—precisely that, an adventurer—a man who had lived by the skin of his teeth. As a youngster he had no specific ambition, no skill or training in any profession.

Errol Flynn's mother told a reporter in New York in 1946 that her famous son had not only been a bad little boy, he had been a nasty little boy. There was little rapport between mother and son; they could never get along together. Flynn resembled his mother in looks and personality, but it was his greatly respected educator father whom he idolized.

As a schoolboy Flynn was rebellious and nonconforming. He excelled in sports, particularly swimming and boxing, but he couldn't, or wouldn't, apply himself to school work. Said Professor Flynn, "There was never a chance of Errol following in my footsteps or taking up any academic career. As far as he was concerned, school

was a place to let off exuberance and not a place where knowledge could be gained."

Flynn attended—due to the influence of his father—a number of excellent schools in England and Australia, but from most of them he was expelled. His first job came in Sydney in September, 1926, when he worked as a clerk for a shipping company. A year later he took off for New Guinea to take up a position as a cadet in the government service, in which capacity he would have been trained as a district officer. The affliction of vacillating interest that had failed him in school now marked his efforts in making a living. He was soon dropped from the government service.

Next came a short period working on a copra plantation as an overseer, and this he left to go into partnership in running a small charter schooner. Eventually, Flynn sold his interest in this enterprise and headed for the gold fields of New Guinea, where he staked a claim at Edey

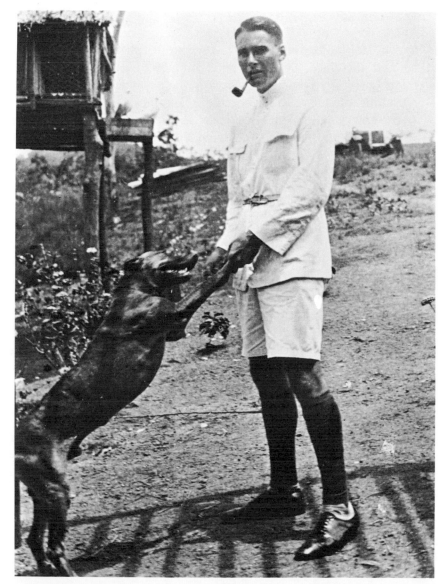

Flynn as a government cadet in New Guinea

Flynn on his boat Sirocco *during his trip along the Great Barrier Reef in 1930*

Creek. He found gold mining less rewarding than he had imagined, so he applied himself to an illicit business he knew would bring money—the recruiting of native labor for the gold mines.

By now a hardened adventurer all of twenty years old, Flynn returned to Sydney and in January, 1930, he invested in a fifty-year-old cutter called *Arop,* which he later re-christened *Sirocco.* With three friends, Flynn decided to sail the boat back to New Guinea, a rash decision in view of the age of the vessel, the inexperience of the crew, and the difficulty of the waters along the Great Barrier Reef. This seven-month voyage was the subject of Flynn's first book, *Beam Ends* (1937).

With his second arrival in New Guinea, Flynn must have pondered the adventurous albeit aimless life he was leading, and he now accepted and held a responsible position as the manager of a tobacco plantation at Laloki. It was also at this period he began earning his first money as a writer, with his columns on New Guinea life for the *Sydney Bulletin.*

Now came the twist of fate that would make all the difference in the life of Errol Flynn. Australian film producer-director Charles Chauvel had seen photographs of Flynn and offered him a part in his film *In the Wake of the Bounty.* Flynn had no experience or prior interest in acting but he was intrigued by the offer and accepted. Discovering an appetite for acting, but unable to find any further acting jobs in Australia, Flynn made his way to England. He arrived in London in the spring of 1933.

Although his only experience had been a part in an obscure Australian film, Flynn now tried to get work in the film studios of London. He found it impossible, but he did hear of an opening in repertory in Northampton. The Northampton Repertory Company was the cradle of Errol Flynn's career as an actor. He stayed with them for a year and a half, and later as an international star he would look back on this period of his life as one of the most rewarding and enjoyable. The people of this dingy industrial town in the English Midlands would never be able to understand this; they would look with envy upon Flynn's fame and wealth and his gay, rollicking life in Hollywood, but for Flynn his stay in Northampton was a plateau of finding and developing himself.

There is a tide in the affairs of men, and Flynn's tide was about to come in. Now an actor with some background, he was able to get work at Warner Brothers' Teddington studio. They offered him a leading part in a routine picture called

16

Flynn as plantation overseer at Laloki, New Guinea, in 1932

Flynn in Hollywood in early 1935 with Marlene Dietrich, Carole Lombard, and Lili Damita

17

Flynn at the beginning of his fame

Murder at Monte Carlo. This proved to be his springboard to Hollywood. Warners put him under contract and he turned up at their Burbank, California, studios at the beginning of 1935. By the end of the year he was firmly established; Warners had gambled on him as Captain Blood and the gamble had paid off handsomely. As part of the great change in his life, Flynn had also taken himself a wife—French film star Lili Damita.

A party was staged after the premiere of *Captain Blood,* and among the guests was veteran director Delmer Daves, then a young writer under contract to Warners. Daves recalls the party struck a tragic note: "Since my lady and I were among the first to arrive, we received the weeping Lili Damita Flynn who begged us again and again, 'Don't . . . please . . . tell him how wonderful he was. . . .' Then more tears as she said over and over (and how true it was), 'Tonight I have lost my husband.' I suppose it did happen that night—for when Errol arrived, boisterously happy, exultant, it was easy to see he meant to enjoy this brave new world that brought him stardom that night. And he did."

The FILMS of
ERROL FLYNN

In the Wake
of the Bounty

1933 An Expeditionary Films Production. Written, produced and directed by Charles Chauvel. Director of Photography: Tasman Higgins. Film Editor: William Shepcrd. Music Director: Lionel Hart. Sound: Arthur Smith and Clive Cross. Narrated by Arthur Greenaway. Running time: 70 minutes.

CAST		
Captain Bligh	Mayne Lynton	
Fletcher Christian	ERROL FLYNN	
The Blind Fiddler	Victor Gourier	
Young	John Warwick	
Isabella	Patricia Penman	

IN 1930, Dr. Herman F. Erben, a combination specialist in tropical diseases, explorer, adventurer, and sometime film-maker, approached Flynn, who at the time was the skipper of a commercial schooner around New Guinea, with a business proposition:

Erben wanted to hire Flynn and his schooner to sail up the fever-ridden, crocodile-infested Sepik River in New Guinea in order to shoot some documentary motion pictures of the headhunters on the shore. Flynn agreed, and during the two-month expedition he was occasionally photographed at the helm or water's edge.

In Sydney, two years later, Charles Chauvel, a producer-director of Australian films, having seen photographs of Flynn, offered him the part of Fletcher Christian in the Australian feature-length picture *In the Wake of the Bounty*.

Flynn worked for three weeks on the film, in his own words, "without the least idea of what I was doing, except that I was supposed to be an actor."

Flynn states in his autobiography that most of his sequences were shot in Maatvai Bay, Tahiti, where 140 years earlier the *Bounty* had anchored. In viewing the film, it is obvious that Flynn's few scenes were shot in a Sydney studio, where the interiors and all of the scenes on the deck of the *Bounty* were staged.

Flynn, for some reason, also states in his autobiography that "Joel Swartz," an American producer, had engaged him for the Sepik River documentary and for *In the Wake of the Bounty*. This name is never mentioned in numerous earlier reports and interviews about the Sepik River expedition, but Erben's name consistently crops up.

To compound the mystery, "Swartz" was the name given in Flynn's 1946 novel, *Showdown,* to a character who charters a schooner to sail up the treacherous Sepik River in order to shoot film of the headhunters! Perhaps Flynn confused his fictional creation with his real-life counterpart, Erben.

In the Wake of the Bounty begins in a tavern

in 1810, where an old salt recalls the history of the *Bounty*. In flashback, Tahitian scenes are shown—including Polynesian dancing—and soon a brief and unexciting mutiny takes place, and the *Bounty* departs Tahiti. The scene dissolves to contemporary Pitcairn Island. The island and its inhabitants—descendants of the mutineers—are explored in some detail. The film closes with a scene depicting a passing ocean liner failing to hear a radio call from Pitcairn for help, obviously meant to symbolize the island's rugged isolation.

Mr. and Mrs. Chauvel and photographer Tasman Higgins landed the first motion picture camera on Pitcairn Island to film the sequences that comprise the majority of the footage.

Pitcairn and the scenes on Tahiti are handled well, with the film generating some real interest in the strange lineage of the Pitcairn Islanders and their difficult existence. The documentary aspect of the film is certainly its only redeeming feature, for the "historical" section is undramatic, static, and amateurish.

Made soon after the advent of sound, *In the Wake of the Bounty*'s sound track, consisting of stock sea chanties and Hawaiian music supplemented with overabundant commentary, is pretty grim.

Tasman Higgins' camera work was generally praised as the highlight of the production, but *Variety* in a May 2, 1933, review commented that the acting was "rather patchy." Actually, it was mostly of the scenery-chewing category: deliberate, artificial, and laced with a generous helping of "ham."

In a recent viewing of the film, Flynn, in a blond wig, seemed to contribute the only believable performance of the lot. He had little to do; most of his scenes took place in Bligh's quarters, with Christian looking on as Bligh declaimed.

In the Wake of the Bounty, in its original form, was never theatrically released in the United States. MGM bought the rights when they decided to produce the 1935 *Mutiny on the Bounty,* and some of the documentary footage from the Australian production was incorporated into two nine-minute promotional shorts (*Primitive Pitcairn* and *Pitcairn Island Today*), released by the studio in 1935.

With Mayne Lynton

22

Murder at Monte Carlo

1935   A Warner Brothers First National Production. Directed by Ralph Ince. Screenplay by Michael Barringer. Based on a story by Tom Van Dycke. Director of Photography: Basil Emmott. Art Director: G. H. Ward. Running time: 70 minutes.

CAST
Gilian	Eve GRAY
Dyter	Errol FLYNN
Dr. Heinrich Becker	Paul GRAETZ
Collum	Lawrence Hanray
Marc Orton	Ellis Irving
Major	Henry Victor
Yates	Brian Buchel
Duprez	Peter Gawthorne
Margaret Becker	Molly Lamont
Wesley	Gabriel Toyne
Gustav	James Dale
Editor	Henry Longhurst
Sankey	Ernest Sefton

BY late 1934, Flynn had been acting in England about a year and a half, mostly with the Northampton Repertory Company. Managing to dash between theaters, he was able to play small parts in two plays that were simultaneously appearing in London's West End in the evening while looking for film work during the day.

According to Irving Asher, who at the time was managing director of the Warner Brothers First National studios in Teddington, near London, Flynn, by persistence, managed to finagle an interview with Asher. Impressed with his physical attributes, personality, and intelligence, Asher placed Flynn under contract without even seeing him on the screen or waiting for a test, and sent a cable to Warners in Burbank in October, 1934. It read:

> Signed today seven years' optional contract best picture bet we have ever seen. He twenty-five Irish looks cross between Charles Farrell and George Brent same type and build excellent actor champion boxer swimmer guarantee he real find.

Three days after the interview a leading man was urgently needed for a British quota-quickie to be called *Murder at Monte Carlo*. Instead of putting Flynn into small parts at first as planned, Asher risked giving him a lead immediately. He and director Ralph Ince were so impressed with

With Molly Lamont, Peter Gawthorne, and Eve Gray

his work that Asher recommended to Jack Warner that he go to Hollywood immediately upon completion of the film. (During the mid-thirties Asher also recommended that English actors Ian Hunter and Patric Knowles be sent to Warners in Burbank.)

The events described above differ somewhat in detail from the account in Flynn's autobiography (and for that matter in Jack L. Warner's autobiography). However, the circumstances were recalled by the authors many years after the fact, and the Asher version, confirmed by him recently, was from an interview in the *British Film Weekly,* January 9, 1937—less than three years after the incidents took place.

Murder at Monte Carlo was completed in No-vember, 1934, but was not put into general release in England until August, 1935, and did not run at all in the United States. Jack Warner, after the completion of the film, brought Flynn to Hollywood on a six-month contract at $150 a week.

The British *Kinematograph Weekly* in their review of *Murder at Monte Carlo* mentioned that "the film is definitely a cut above the usual quota product. . . . Errol Flynn contributes a high pressure portrayal."

Film Pictorial stated: "There is a fair amount of excitement and the general acting standard is quite good, although, as so often happens in these lesser British films, the dialogue leaves a good deal to be desired."

24

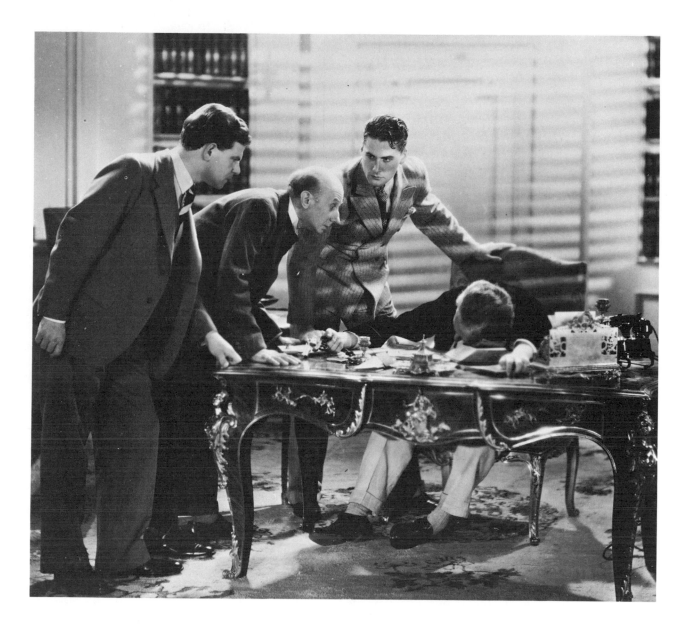

The plot dealt with a newspaper reporter (Flynn) being sent to Monte Carlo to gather details regarding a sensational roulette system, the inventor of which (Graetz) is subsequently discovered mysteriously murdered. The reporter's girl friend (Gray) follows him to Monte Carlo in the hope of obtaining the story for a rival paper. Standard murder mystery ingredients follow—including a reconstruction of the crime at the windup.

The January, 1935, *Monthly Film Bulletin* of the British Film Institute said in part that "Paul Graetz's performance . . . is considerably above the level of the film and serves to emphasize the amateurishness of the rest of the cast. The plot is wildly improbable, the cutting is bad."

Film Weekly of August 9, 1935, referred to the picture as "weakish entertainment on the whole . . . the murder is cleared by Errol Flynn and his sweetheart Eve Gray. The pair act quite charmingly together, but the whole cast suffers from comparison with Paul Graetz's fine performance."

Director-writer Delmer Daves recalls that "Jack Warner asked all of us on writing contracts in Burbank to see the British film which introduced Errol to us for the first time. There was no inkling in it of the Fairbanksian Flynn who developed in America; indeed, he seemed self-conscious. But he *was* the handsome man who was to conquer a few million female hearts, and he was signed based more on that attribute than any evident acting ability."

With Margaret Lindsay

The Case of the Curious Bride

1935   A First National Picture (Warner Bros.). Directed by Michael Curtiz. Associafe Producer: Harry Joe Brown. Screenplay by Tom Reed. Additional Dialogue by Brown Holmes. Based on the novel by Erle Stanley Gardner. Music by Bernhard Kaun. Director of Photography: David Abel. Film Editor: Terry Morse. Art Directors: Carl Jules Weyl and Anton Grot. Sound: Dolph Thomas. Gowns: Orry-Kelly. Special Effects: Fred Jackman and Fred Jackman, Jr. Assistant Director: Jack Sullivan. Running time: 80 minutes.

CAST
Perry Mason	WARREN WILLIAM
Rhoda Montaine	Margaret LINDSAY
Carl Montaine	Donald WOODS
Della Street	Claire DODD
Spudsy	Allen JENKINS
Dr. Claude Millbeck	Philip Reed
Joe Lucas	Barton MacLane
Doris Pender	Winifred Shaw
Oscar Pender	Warren Hymer
Coroner Wilbur Strong	Olin Howland
G. Phillip Montaine	Charles Richman
Toots Howard	Thomas Jackson
Gregory Moxley	Errol Flynn
Byrd (Detective)	Robert Gleckler
Fritz (Detective)	James Donlan
Florabelle Morgan	Mayo Methot
Luigi	George Humbert
District Attorney Stacey	Henry Kolker
Fibo Morgan	Paul Hurst

WHEN Flynn arrived in Hollywood early in 1935, he was not immediately thrust into leading roles. Just another young, hopeful contract player, he was slated for a part in *A Midsummer Night's Dream*, but instead his first opportunity in an American picture was limited

indeed. In *The Case of the Curious Bride* he had two scenes: In the first he was seen as a corpse in silhouette only; in the second, he appeared briefly (approximately sixty seconds)—with no dialogue—in a flashback near the conclusion of the film. His exposure in this film was hardly guaranteed to open the doors of stardom.

The Case of the Curious Bride was the second of four Warner film versions of the Perry Mason murder mystery novels with Warren William as the original Perry. A good cut above most B pictures of the time, and following in the tradition of *The Thin Man* the year before, it combined mystery, humor, sleuthing, and clever legal quirks, and managed to lace a fairly interesting plot with crisp dialogue and swift pacing. The book's lengthy courtroom scenes were eliminated, and comic relief was added.

Lawyer Mason's help is sought by an old friend, Rhoda Montaine (Lindsay), who tells him that her first husband Gregory Moxley (Flynn), whom she thought dead, has reappeared, complicating her relations with her second husband (Woods), a millionaire's son. When Mason goes to see Moxley, he discovers him murdered, with Rhoda's

keys by his side. Mason then tries to ferret out the truth, save his client, and outwit the police and district attorney. He eventually brings all the suspects together at a cocktail party (the murder-mystery obligatory scene), during which the real killer (Woods) of Rhoda's first husband confesses.

In the ensuing flashback, Rhoda goes to see Moxley to refuse his blackmailing scheme. Moxley, incensed, slaps her about the room, but she picks up a poker and strikes him. Meanwhile, her second husband has followed her to Moxley's, and after she has left, he and Moxley have a violent fight, resulting in Moxley falling against the sharp, knifelike edge of a piece of mirror, broken during the struggle, which kills him.

Margaret Lindsay was thus the first actress with whom Flynn worked in Hollywood. She recalls that during the slapping and poker pummeling he accidentally knocked her out. Terribly contrite, he later apologized over and over.

Many of the exteriors in *The Case of the Curious Bride* were shot in San Francisco. All of the film was given slick treatment by Michael Curtiz, Warners' top director and the man who would direct Flynn in eleven subsequent films, including many of his best.

Don't Bet on Blondes

1935 A Warner Brothers Picture. Directed by Robert Florey. Associate Producer: Samuel Bischoff. Original Screenplay by Isabel Dawn and Boyce DeGaw. Director of Photography: William Rees. Dialogue Director: Arthur Greville Collins. Film Editor: Thomas Richards. Art Director: Esdras Hartley. Musical Director: Leo F. Forbstein. Assistant Director: Eric Stacey. Running time: 60 minutes.

CAST *"Odds" Owen*　　WARREN WILLIAM
Colonel Jefferson Davis Youngblood
　　　　　　　　GUY KIBBEE

Marilyn Young	Claire DODD
"Numbers"	William GARGAN
"Brains"	Vince Barnett
Philbert O. Slemp	Hobart Cavanaugh
T. Everett Markham	Clay Clement
David Van Dusen	Errol Flynn
"Doc"	Spencer Charters
Dwight Boardman	Walter Byron
Steve	Eddie Shubert
J. Mortimer Slade	Jack Norton
Switchboard Operator	Mary Treen
Ella Purdy	Maude Eburne
Professor Friedrich Wilhelm Gruber	
	Herman Bing

With Frank Moran, Vince Barnett, Constantine Romanoff, Ben F. Hendricks, Jack Pennick, Jack Low, and Marc Lawrence

IN this minor and undistinguished B picture, Warren William played a big-time gambler who starts a kind of American Lloyd's of London and insures a wealthy Kentucky colonel (Kibbee) against the possibility that his actress daughter (Dodd) will stop being the source of his income by marrying. William takes a personal interest, falls in love with the young lady, and after the usual complications, marries her just before the fade-out.

Flynn fared better than in *The Case of the Curious Bride*. He played a society playboy who also falls in love with Kibbee's daughter but is eliminated from the running by William's ploys. His two scenes, occurring more than halfway through the picture, take place on a golf course and in a night club—both with the very pretty Miss Dodd. Other than looking very young, lean, and handsome and displaying boyish charm, there was little opportunity to indicate a powerful potential, since his total screen time in this opus was approximately five minutes.

Captain Blood

With Olivia de Havilland

1935 A Cosmopolitan Production; A First National Picture (Warner Bros.). Directed by Michael Curtiz. Executive Producer: Hal B. Wallis. Associate Producers: Harry Joe Brown and Gordon Hollingshead. Screenplay by Casey Robinson. Based on the novel by Rafael Sabatini. Music by Erich Wolfgang Korngold. Director of Photography: Hal Mohr. Additional photography: Ernest Haller. Dialogue Director: Stanley Logan. Film Editor: George Amy. Art Director: Anton Grot. Sound: C. A. Riggs. Gowns: Milo Anderson. Special Effects: Fred Jackman. Orchestrations: Hugo Friedhofer and Ray Heindorf. Assistant Director: Sherry Shourds. Fencing Master: Fred Cavens. Running time: 119 minutes.

CAST
Peter Blood	ERROL FLYNN
Arabella Bishop	OLIVIA de HAVILLAND
Colonel Bishop	Lionel ATWILL
Captain Levasseur	Basil RATHBONE
Jeremy Pitt	Ross ALEXANDER
Hagthorpe	Guy KIBBEE
Lord Willoughby	Henry STEPHENSON
Wolverstone	Robert Barrat
Dr. Bronson	Hobart Cavanaugh
Dr. Whacker	Donald Meek
Mrs. Barlowe	Jessie Ralph
Honesty Nuttall	Forrester Harvey
Reverend Ogle	Frank McGlynn, Sr.
Captain Gardner	Holmes Herbert
Andrew Baynes	David Torrence
Cahusac	J. Carrol Naish
Don Diego	Pedro de Cordoba
Governor Steed	George Hassell
Kent	Harry Cording
Baron Jeffreys	Leonard Mudie
Prosecutor	Ivan Simpson
Captain Hobart	Stuart Casey
Lord Gildoy	Denis d'Auburn
Mrs. Steed	Mary Forbes
Court Clerk	E. E. Clive
Lord Chester Dyke	Colin Kenny
Mrs. Baynes	Maude Leslie
Branded Slave	Gardner James
King James	Vernon Steele

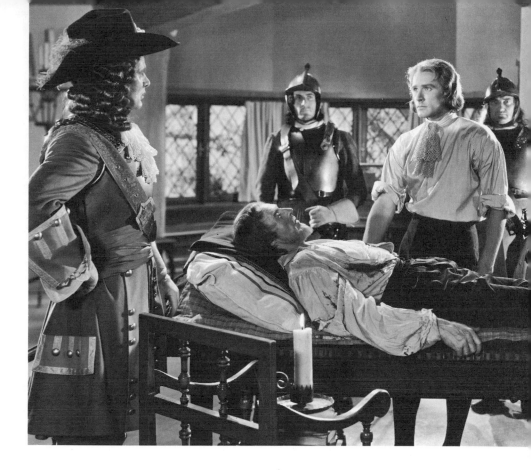

In 1934 two films were released that set the stage for a revival of the swashbuckling costume romance, so popular and abundant during the 1920s, but dormant after the introduction of sound and during the early Depression years. *Treasure Island* and *The Count of Monte Cristo* also were "immortal classics" and indicative of Hollywood's renewed literary preoccupation.

Encouraged by the success of the period adventure films, MGM went ahead with plans for a lavish *Mutiny on the Bounty* (1935) and Warners definitely decided to produce *Captain Blood*, a property they had acquired along with the Vitagraph Company some years before. Vitagraph's 1923 silent version of Rafael Sabatini's novel featured J. Warren Kerrigan as the redoubtable

With Ross Alexander

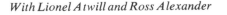

With Lionel Atwill and Ross Alexander

Peter Blood, physician, humanist, and buccaneer *par excellence*.

Robert Donat had played the Count of Monte Cristo and seemed a likely choice for Captain Blood in the remake. However, due to some confusion in contractual negotiations between London and Burbank, Donat dropped out at the last minute and Warners needed an exceptional leading man fast.

With Errol Flynn, it was a question of the right man being in the right place at the right time. Jack L. Warner had director Michael Curtiz, who had used Flynn in *The Case of the Curious Bride,* test the newcomer in a key scene. As a result of the test, he had the part hands down. Olivia de Havilland, a young member of Max Reinhardt's touring *A Midsummer Night's Dream* company who had been carried over to the 1935 Warner film version, was given a major opportunity to co-star with the virtually unknown Flynn. Warner contract player Jean Muir was originally set to play opposite Donat.

The screenplay was a reasonably faithful adaptation of Sabatini's 1922 novel: During the reign of James II (*circa* 1688), one of England's most unpopular kings, a young physician by the name of Peter Blood is found treating a wounded rebel. Summarily convicted of treason, he is sent to Jamaica to be sold into slavery. After Blood suc-

32

cessfully treats the governor's gout, he is granted special privileges. During this time Blood falls in love with Arabella Bishop (de Havilland), the niece of a plantation owner (Atwill).

When Spanish pirates cannonade and capture the town, Blood and a group of slaves escape to the buccaneers' craft and become pirates themselves. Numerous adventures in the Caribbean follow, including an association with a French pirate (Rathbone) that ends in a duel-to-the-death, with Blood walking away with the bone of contention—Arabella. (The duel gives only a suggestion of the excellent swordplay in later Flynn epics.)

Later, with Britain at war with France and James II ousted by William of Orange, Blood receives a navy commission, defeats two French ships in an exciting battle, and is appointed Jamaica's governor—with Arabella at his side.

Warners approached this spectacle with great care. Always economy minded, the studio decided upon a way to minimize the expenses hitherto inherent in period sea pictures. Too often full-scale and expensive ships had been built and manned, then sent to sea with an expensive cast and technical crew, only to sail up and down the Pacific looking for the right weather—while the overhead mounted. In *Captain Blood* there were naval battles, bombardments, and the sinking of two ships to consider.

With Robert Barrat

With Yola d'Avril and Basil Rathbone

33

With J. Carrol Naish, Basil Rathbone, Guy Kibbee, Ross Alexander, and Robert Barrat

The plan was to combine process shots and miniatures with regular sets, backlot, and location work near Laguna Beach for the duel. On occasion, a few clips were lifted from the Vitagraph *Captain Blood* and the 1924 *Sea Hawk,* produced by First National, a company that had been acquired by Warner Brothers.

For the 1935 *Captain Blood* no full-scale ships were used; even the town of Port Royal was miniature, to a considerable degree. The small-scale ships shot in a studio tank were approximately eighteen feet long with sixteen-foot masts. The dramatic action aboard ship was filmed on one of the sound stages, where the main deck of the ship was re-created.

Flynn, considering his limited acting experience, did an exceptional job. It was wide-open gallantry, but the fervor was nicely tempered with utter sincerity and a somewhat impudent charm, thereby laying the groundwork for the essential Flynn acting style. His pairing with the young, pert, and lovely de Havilland seemed to produce the right screen chemistry.

Flynn was quite nervous during the first days

With Basil Rathbone

of shooting, and his performance reflected this. As he gained confidence, his acting improved considerably; so much so that later on the first two week's footage was filmed again.

During the shooting of one of the action scenes on board the ship, Flynn collapsed from a recurrence of malaria, originally contracted by the actor in New Guinea.

Captain Blood opened in December, 1935 (six weeks following *Mutiny on the Bounty*), to generally excellent reviews. The public took to the film, Flynn, and de Havilland immediately. Swashbucklers—old-fashioned "moving" pictures—were once again in, and Warners had the only first-rate swashbuckler to handle the assignments.

Captain Blood also served to introduce to filmgoers the talents of the highly esteemed Austrian composer Erich Wolfgang Korngold. This was his first original film score. Korngold had been brought to Hollywood in 1934 by his friend and associate, the impresario Max Reinhardt, to arrange and conduct the Mendelssohn score for Reinhardt's and Warners' film version of *A Midsummer Night's Dream*. He later accepted a contract from Warners, and thus became the first composer of international reputation to be con-

tracted to a Hollywood film studio on a multipicture basis. The excellence of his film scores had considerable influence on the development of this form of composition.

Captain Blood was nationally reissued in December, 1951, following the enthusiastic response to Warners' *Captain Horatio Hornblower* (1951), a picture announced many times for Flynn, starting as far back as 1939, but eventually filmed with Gregory Peck in the title role.

On seeing *Captain Blood* today, it must be noted that the film dates more than the subsequent *Robin Hood* and *The Sea Hawk*. The dialogue tends to be flowery and the physical production is a bit tacky here and there—despite the ingenuity of miniatures, process, and so forth. Nevertheless, it served nicely to springboard Flynn's upcoming costume productions that were to be more finished and opulent.

Captain Blood was a "first" on several counts: it was the film that established Flynn's swashbuckler image; his first starring role; his first appearance with de Havilland, who was to be his co-star in seven other films; his first film scored by Korngold, who was to score six subsequent Flynn films; and his first starring film with direc-

tor Michael Curtiz, who would direct eight subsequent Flynn films, in addition to countless other big pictures such as *Angels with Dirty Faces, Yankee Doodle Dandy, Casablanca,* and *Mildred Pierce.*

Shortly after completing *Captain Blood,* Flynn appeared in a Technicolor short subject, *Pirate Party on Catalina Isle,* along with his wife, Lili Damita, and several other stars, including Marion Davies, Cary Grant, Virginia Bruce, John Gilbert, and Lee Tracy. Chester Morris acted as master of ceremonies, and music, featuring the song "Avalon," was provided by Charles (Buddy) Rogers and his band. Written by Alexander Van Dorn and produced by Louis Lewyn, this two-reel featurette was released by MGM early in 1936.

With Lionel Atwill and Olivia de Havilland

Part Two

The Pinnacle Era

At a Los Angeles tennis tournament in September, 1936,
with Lili Damita

While making The Prince and the Pauper, *Flynn looks over his newly published book* Beam Ends

THE pinnacle years for Errol Flynn were 1936 to 1942. With *Captain Blood* he became a star of the first magnitude; the world-wide success of that film took Flynn from obscurity to fame in one gigantic leap. The young adventurer who had lived by his wits and occasionally skirted the borders of larceny to make a living was now well paid, adulated by a large public, and cultivated by his studio, Warner Brothers.

The deciding vote on using Flynn in *Captain Blood* belonged to studio boss Jack L. Warner. In his autobiography, *My First Hundred Years in Hollywood,* Warner says, "I wonder whether The Baron, as I called him, would have turned down that chance if he could have forseen the sordid and troublesome road ahead. I doubt it. He had to live as he lived." Despite their differences, Warner expressed more of a fondness for Flynn than for the other actors on his payroll. Perhaps he saw in Flynn, as did so many people, something of himself. Says Warner, "To the Walter Mittys of the world he was all the heroes in one

magnificent, sexy, animal package. I just wish we had someone around today half as good as Flynn."

Errol Flynn was in every respect a natural subject for film stardom. A fine athlete, he excelled as a swimer, boxer, and tennis player, and because of the demands of his work he quickly became an accomplished horseman and fencer. He moved with catlike agility. His attractiveness was both his blessing and his curse; it made it easy for him to succeed in films but it also trapped him. The Handsome Hero, noble and dashing, was the obvious assignment for Errol Flynn. This is what the fans wanted and this is what Warner Brothers gave them. In those early years his screen image and his personal life were closely allied; everyone expected the good-looking, young actor with the devil-may-care air to behave much the same off-screen as on. And he did.

The publicists at Warner Brothers found themselves with a peculiar problem: instead of having to invent an interesting background for a new actor they had to present Flynn in a credible light.

39

Nothing that a publicist could imagine could match what Flynn had actually done in the ten years prior to his arrival in Hollywood. Many of the publicists were dubious, but with time corroboration leaked in. Much of what was corroborated proved embarrassing to the studio; they learned that their actor had indeed done adventurous things, quite a few of them nefarious, and that there were places in which Flynn was far from highly regarded.

It was said that if Flynn ever went back to New Guinea he would either be shot by people he had cheated or imprisoned by the government for his activities in slave trading. Flynn never returned to either New Guinea or Australia. In a Christmas message broadcast to Australia, he added something not in the script: "If there's anyone listening to whom I owe money, I'm prepared to forget about it if you are."

While he enjoyed being a film star and the life it enabled him to live, Flynn resented being merchandised. In time he worked up a considerable dislike for Hollywood, particularly its moguls. From his home off Mulholland Drive, atop one of the Hollywood hills, Flynn could look out, on a smogless day, and see some miles in the distance Forest Lawn Cemetery, where many of filmdom's greats are buried. He once pointed to it and said to Nora Eddington, his second wife, "For God's sake, don't ever bury me there." Ironically, it was exactly the place where he would be buried.

The beauty of face and form that made Flynn's ascent to stardom so easy and then trapped him, had a parallel in his private life. There, too, his personality and his looks made everything easy for him. All kinds of people wanted to know him and enjoy his company. His opportunities for pleasure were limitless, and this, coupled with an inordinate capacity for hedonism, set up a pattern that lasted the remainder of his life.

Errol Flynn garnered himself a reputation as a ladies' man, as a twentieth-century Casanova, as a man with an unusually cultivated interest in women. Flynn accepted this image just as he accepted the role of celluloid hero, and in time he became a kind of comic phallic figure. Flynn even seemed to encourage these images, and he laughed about them along with everybody else. How he actually felt is another matter. Along the Hollywood grapevine it was rumored that Flynn was a man of quite ordinary sexuality, and a splendid

Flynn with the director of most of his best films, Michael Curtiz

lover only when he was genuinely interested in a woman. His charming manners and the devilish look in his eyes doubtless led women to believe he was something more. The fact that Flynn was once tried on charges of rape amused his carousing friends, who thought it as ridiculous as a man accused of eating at a banquet.

Flynn was married three times. His first wife was the French film actress Lili Damita, whom he met on the ship that brought him to America at the end of 1934. They were married in June of the following year. Lili Damita was frequently asked what it was like being married to Flynn. She told a magazine writer in 1939, "I do not depend on Flynn for the things women usually expect of their husbands." She went on to explain—somewhat laughingly—that he was never on time, that he forgot appointments, that he didn't attend to business details, and that he was undemonstrative. She added that she loved him anyway and that he was, as everyone suspected, an endearing rascal. Damita said she had learned,

40

through a sometimes painful process, that the only way to deal with Flynn was to let him have his own way. But she found, as did his other wives, that he was paradoxical and slightly perverse, especially in his humor, "You never know when he is telling the truth. He lies for the fun of it."

The Flynn-Damita marriage lasted seven years but it was pitted with constant quarrels and separations and bad publicity. Damita was a volatile, tempestuous, jealous woman, and Flynn was a man with little or no interest in being married. They divorced in 1942 and Damita was granted an alimony of $1,500 a month, tax free, plus a half interest in all his properties. Flynn was ready to pay that sum at the time, but as the years went by he grew bitter about the constant drain on his finances, and in the last ten years of his life, when his income was spotty, he was always behind in his payments. From the marriage to Damita came Flynn's only son, Sean. Damita didn't marry again until after Flynn died.

Everything seemed to come easily to Errol Flynn in his pinnacle years—including trouble and controversy. He was the answer to a journalist's dream, always involved in escapades and brawls, always good for a laugh. In early 1937 he went to Spain to take a close look at the Civil War, claiming he had a commission to act as a war correspondent. He made the headlines from Spain with the news that he had been killed in battle, but like the report of Mark Twain's death, the news was greatly exaggerated.

One of Flynn's closest friends at the start of his Hollywood career was David Niven, a young Scotsman who had been a British army officer, and after resigning his commission, had proceeded to adventure in the world. He and Flynn were similar in many respects, both being British gentlemen with crazy-quilt backgrounds and pronounced appetites for high living. Niven looks back on that first year of friendship with Flynn with strong nostalgia. "He was an enchanting creature. I had more fun with Errol than everybody else put together. We shared a house on the beach at Malibu and called it Cirrhosis-by-the-Sea. It was never-ending fun."

Errol Flynn tried to get into the Second World War but he was rejected by every branch of the armed services because of his health. Some people, including David Niven, feel this rejection had a profound effect on Flynn and that his heroic

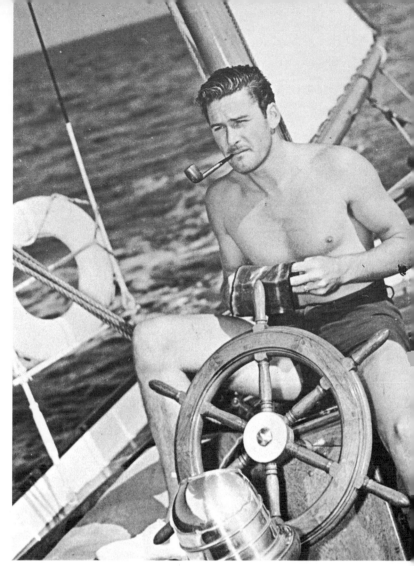

Flynn on his ketch Sirocco

screen image caused the actor an inner suffering. Flynn was, at this time, still a spectacular athlete and he looked to be in fine condition. But his draft rating was 4F, and it became known that he had an "athletic heart." It was also discovered, but not revealed, that Flynn suffered from recurrent malaria, a hangover from his days in New Guinea, and that he also had a measure of tuberculosis.

"I went off to the war in 1939," says Niven, "and I really think Errol suffered because he didn't. He'd done a lot of films about war and these were sometimes laughed at, especially in England. He was parodied as a man who should have been in it, and he was most unfairly pilloried because of it. This ate into him. This, compounded with the fact that there was a great place—the war itself—for heroics at that time."

The things that bothered Flynn he kept to himself: his marital problems, his film heroics, the typecasting, and the fact that hardly anyone took

was a wartime divertissement and regarded as almost comic relief from the war news. It was, however, no enjoyment for Flynn, whose appearance during the protracted arraignment changed from robust to wan; his tan faded and his face became drawn. He realized a prison term awaited him if proven guilty, and he later admitted he had made an arrangement with a private aviator to fly him out of the country immediately had he not been acquitted.

It was Flynn's belief that the Los Angeles district attorney had made him a scapegoat for Hollywood in order to discipline the film community. Some of the evidence presented gave reason to wonder, and it is possible that neither of the two girls would have made charges had they not been encouraged to do so.

The trial cost Flynn $50,000, thirty thousand of it going to Giesler—a lesser fee than he had charged other celebrities. Giesler considered Flynn an excellent witness and thought that his gentlemanly demeanor throughout the trial had been an important factor. One aspect puzzled Flynn: "Jerry never at any time asked me whether I was guilty or innocent."

Warner Brothers were fearful lest Flynn's trial affect his power at the box office. They soon found his popularity not only had held but had a new spurt of interest. A new phrase was added to the English language: "In like Flynn." He was now fair game for the comedians; even the titles of his films at this period of his career lent themselves to double entendre—*They Died with Their Boots On, Desperate Journey, Edge of Darkness* and *Thank Your Lucky Stars.* One journalist wag suggested that since Flynn had been accused of making love while wearing his socks, Warners should release *Gentleman Jim* simply as *Jim.*

But the crest had been reached; if Flynn had not been taken seriously before the trial he was even less respected now. Most of his really fine films were behind him. He made a few interesting films in the years that followed, but much of his own interest began to lag, his health didn't allow him to be quite so dashing, and the studio chieftains were content so long as he played the part of Errol Flynn. His first seven years in the movies were the best years.

him seriously. Then in November, 1942, something happened that changed his life and made a difference to his image. Charged with statutory rape, Flynn was arrested and brought to trial.

Flynn was tried and acquitted, but the acquittal was not the real issue. The public rightly assumed that where there was smoke there was also fire, and Flynn was revealed as a man who had been flagrantly indiscreet and careless in his affairs. Having ridden high and wide most of his life, Flynn now found himself in a humiliating spotlight. The trial was a legal conundrum; the predicament of a man charged with having had sexual intercourse with two girls who were under the legal California age of consent—eighteen. Both girls had dubious backgrounds, and it was this that enabled Flynn's ace lawyer, the late Jerry Giesler, to swing the trial in his favor. The trial

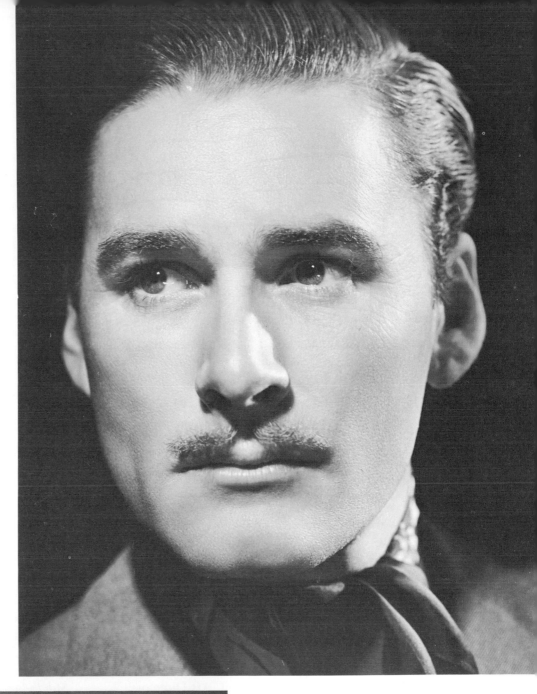

Flynn, age thirty, and at the height of his popularity

Flynn in January, 1943, at the rape trial, with his lawyers Bob Ford and Jerry Giesler

43

The Charge of the Light Brigade

1936 A Warner Brothers Picture. Directed by Michael Curtiz. Executive Producer: Hal B. Wallis. Associate Producer: Samuel Bischoff. Screenplay by Michel Jacoby and Rowland Leigh. Based on an original story by Michel Jacoby. Music by Max Steiner. Director of Photography: Sol Polito. Dialogue Director: Stanley Logan. Film Editor: George Amy. Art Director: John Hughes. Sound: C. A. Riggs. Gowns: Milo Anderson. Special Effects: Fred Jackman and H. F. Koenekamp. Orchestrations: Hugo Friedhofer. Assistant Director: Jack Sullivan. Director of horse action: B. Reeves Eason. Technical Adviser: Captain E. Rochfort-John. Technical Adviser of military drills and tactics: Major Sam Harris. Running time: 115 minutes.

CAST *Major Geoffrey Vickers* ERROL FLYNN
Elsa Campbell
OLIVIA de HAVILLAND
Captain Perry Vickers Patric KNOWLES
Sir Charles Macefield
Henry STEPHENSON

Sir Benjamin Warrenton	Nigel BRUCE
Colonel Campbell	Donald CRISP
Captain Randall	David NIVEN
Surat Khan	C. Henry Gordon
Major Jowett	G. P. Huntley, Jr.
Count Igor Volonoff	Robert Barrat
Lady Octavia Warrenton	Spring Byington
Sir Humphrey Harcourt	E. E. Clive
Subahdar-Major Puran Singh	
	J. Carrol Naish
Cornet Barclay	Walter Holbrook
Cornet Pearson	Charles Sedgwick
Prema Singh	Scotty Beckett
Colonel Woodward	Lumsden Hare
Prema's Mother	Princess Baigum
Wazir	George Regas
Major Anderson	Colin Kenny
Colonel Coventry	Gordon Hart
Mrs. Jowett	Helen Sanborn
General O'Neill	Holmes Herbert
General Dunbar	Boyd Irwin
Bentham	Reginald Sheffield
General Canrobert	Georges Renavent
Lord Cardigan	Charles Croker King
Lord Raglan	Brandon Hurst

With David Niven, E. E. Clive, Walter Holbrook, and Charles Sedgwick

OF the many films produced about the British Empire holding forth in northern Africa and India during the imperialistic Victorian years, *The Charge of the Light Brigade* ranks as one of the best. *The Lives of a Bengal Lancer* (1935) was the first in the cycle during the mid-thirties; *The Four Feathers* (1939) took advantage of Technicolor, actual locales in the Sudan, and a better plot; *Gunga Din* (1939) had more fun with its leading characters and treated early battle scenes as a romp; but *The Charge* held its own in the areas of fine casting, large-scale production, and brilliantly staged action sequences.

While in China as news correspondent for the New York *World*, a young reporter named Michel Jacoby first decided that the famous charge would be a marvelous subject for films. He may or may not have been aware that the historical incident had been utilized for a one-reel motion picture as early as 1912. A British film of 1930 called *Balaclava* also had dealt with the charge, but otherwise the subject hadn't been touched by any studio.

Jacoby seriously began collecting facts regarding the Crimean War. Several years later, in 1934, he put his story behind the disastrous blunder on paper, and for a year tried to sell the idea in Hollywood. When Paramount's *Lives of a Bengal Lancer*—which had been sitting around for years prior to production—was well received, Warners decided to purchase Jacoby's idea. As things developed, all the fact-finding that had occupied Jacoby for years was thrown out, and instead an invented narrative with fabricated characters in *India* (à la *Bengal Lancers*) was used for the main portions of the film. It was evidently thought that the people and events behind the relatively obscure Crimean War of 1853-56 would hardly be of interest to contemporary American audiences.

The story of Warners' *Charge,* which echoes Kipling more than Tennyson, goes this way: Surat Khan (Gordon), a fictitious character devised as an unprincipled but influential chieftain of India in 1850, is cut off from a handsome annuity from England, and as a consequence enters a secret alliance with Russia. Because trouble is brewing in the Balkans between Russia on the one hand,

With Walter Holbrook, E. E. Clive, David Niven, and C. Henry Gordon

45

With Donald Crisp and Olivia de Havilland

and Turkey, France, and England on the other, Major Geoffrey Vickers of the British 27th Lancers (Flynn), stationed in India, is sent to Arabia to purchase thousands of horses for the British Army. En route he stops at Calcutta, where he meets his fiancée (de Havilland) and his brother, Perry (Knowles). Perry and Geoffrey's fiancée have fallen in love, but she feels duty-bound to marry Geoffrey, to whom she has been engaged for some time.

Surat Khan, determined to settle a score, later destroys the garrison of the 27th Lancers at Chukoti. Fortunately, Geoffrey and his fiancée, who had recently returned to the fort, manage to escape the massacre.

The 27th Lancers are then transferred to the Crimea. Here Geoffrey learns that Surat Khan is with the Russians, and in order to avenge the slaughter of the men, women, and children at Chukoti, he substitutes one dispatch for another, ordering the brigade not to retreat, but to advance and charge a Russian body of about 25,000 infantry with artillery and cavalry. So into the Valley of Death rode close to seven hundred British soldiers. Over two-thirds were killed, but Surat Khan is finished by a lance thrown by Geoffrey just before he too dies.

A chain of reasons and mistakes were behind the imbroglio of the orders for the actual charge, but none of these was even hinted at in the film's

With C. Henry Gordon, Robert Barrat, and Henry Stephenson

The attack on Chukoti

With Scotty Beckett

totally false narrative. Lord Raglan and Lord Cardigan, two major historical figures, were reduced to bit parts and shown as not being implicated at all in the order and execution of the charge.

By making revenge the motive in the script for the futile gallantry, the film glorifies militarism and vindicates insubordination. On these counts it is absurd, and the false heroics are difficult to take seriously today. But, if one looks at it merely as a great show, a spectacle, and can click back to boyhood delight in exotic adventure, stalwart gentlemen, evil amirs, and glorious death, then—and only then—can *The Charge of the Light Bri-*

With Patric Knowles

gade be met and thoroughly enjoyed on its own terms.

The Charge was expensive ($1,200,000), and every penny shows on the screen. A complete British fort (the Chukoti garrison) was constructed at Agoura (Lasky Mesa), west of the San Fernando Valley. A leopard hunt was staged at nearby Lake Sherwood, and many exteriors were photographed at Lone Pine, California, Hollywood's perennial substitute for India. Chatsworth in the San Fernando Valley was the locale for the final charge with additional horse action and falls photographed near Sonora in Northern California.

An exceptional piece of film-making by any standard, the lengthy charge is still one of a relatively few major action sequences that can be regarded as classic. The succession of images that come to mind include the low tracking shots of the horses increasing their tempo from a stately gait to a full gallop, the dynamic intercutting of singled-out detail showing men and horses falling, cannon roaring by the lens, lancers leaping over the camera in pit shots, a wounded soldier caught in his stirrup and being dragged in the dust, buglers reiterating the charge, closeups of Flynn waving his saber and shouting "Onward, men!" wide panoramic composition of the mass action, individual combat with swords, lances, and smoke filling the screen.

Curtiz worked with B. Reeves (Breezy) Eason, noted second-unit and action specialist, in directing this matchless mayhem. It is difficult to say who was responsible for what, but it is unfair to give full credit to Eason, as has been done on occasion, since people associated with the film have stated that Curtiz was very much involved in the handling of this sequence.

One negative note regarding the use of "The running W": This was an insensitive and brutal method utilized years ago to force a horse to trip on cue. Wires were attached to bands on a horse's front legs; these wires fused into one directly under his chest, and it was of whatever length necessary for the run, with the end firmly attached to a post in the ground. When the wire would run out and was snapped taut, the horse would buckle headfirst and very often be seriously hurt, which necessitated killing the animal. The wholesale use of this miserable device in *The Charge* caused humane groups in general and the Society for the Prevention of Cruelty to Animals in particular rightfully to complain. Henceforth, for the most part, other methods with little or no danger to the horses were put into practice in the United States.

As for Flynn, he performed in a very British, sincere, and charming manner. In his autobiography he states that this was by far the most difficult picture he made in terms of a long, hard

shooting schedule, weather problems, and difficult action.

Although Anita Louise was scheduled up until the last moment to provide the feminine interest, she was replaced by Olivia.

Warners never nationally reissued *The Charge* after World War II as they did with so many of Flynn's big action pictures of the thirties. Perhaps the glorification and justification of imperialistic conquest, and the revenge motive for the final sacrifice of some five hundred men seemed a little out of keeping with postwar attitudes. Then, too, the frightful display of the falling horses would have left the studio open to renewed criticisms.

Among the many merits of *The Charge of the Light Brigade* was the music score by Max Steiner. This was his first score for Warner Brothers, and from then on his career was mainly with that studio. It was Steiner, more than any other person, who realized the potential of original music scoring in films. He became the pioneer of this new avenue for composers in the early thirties, and years later he would be affectionately referred to as "the grand old man of movie music."

It is worthy of note that Errol Flynn received excellent musical support; most of his best films were scored either by Steiner or Erich Korngold. Steiner did fifteen of Flynn's pictures, including seven of his eight Westerns. The composer preferred scoring dramatic love stories, like those for Bette Davis, but in point of fact his skill in providing suitable music to the exciting Flynn vehicles was a not inconsiderable factor in their over-all effectiveness.

50

With Anita Louise and Sir Cedric Hardwicke

Green Light

1937 A Cosmopolitan Production; A First National Picture (Warner Bros.). Directed by Frank Borzage. Executive Producer: Hal B. Wallis. Associate Producer: Henry Blanke. Screenplay by Milton Krims. Based on the novel by Lloyd C. Douglas. Music by Max Steiner. Director of Photography: Byron Haskin. Film Editor: James Gibbon. Art Director: Max Parker. Sound: Robert B. Lee. Gowns: Orry-Kelly. Special Effects: Fred Jackman, Jr., H. F. Koenekamp, and Willard Van Enger. Orchestrations: Hugo Friedhofer. Assistant Director: Lew Borzage. Running time: 85 minutes.

CAST

Dr. Newell Paige	ERROL FLYNN
Phyllis Dexter	Anita LOUISE
Frances Ogilvie	Margaret LINDSAY
Dean Harcourt	Sir Cedric HARDWICKE
Dr. John Stafford	Walter ABEL
Dr. Endicott	Henry O'Neill
Mrs. Dexter	Spring Byington
Pat Arlen	Erin O'Brien-Moore
Dr. Lane	Henry Kolker
Dr. Booth	Pierre Watkin
Sheriff	Granville Bates
Sheepman	Russell Simpson
Nurse	Myrtle Stedman

St. Luke's Choristers

With Margaret Lindsay and Anita Louise

51

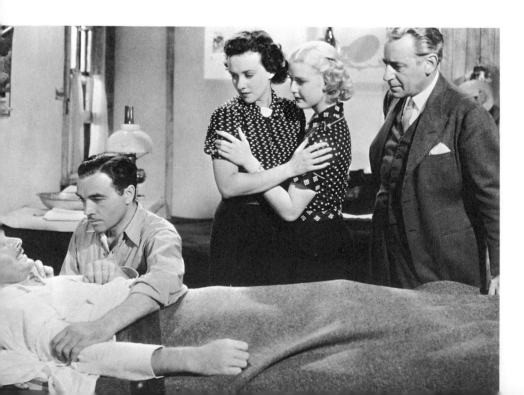

With Walter Abel

AN idealistic young surgeon (Flynn) sacrifices his career rather than place the blame for a fatal surgical slip where it belongs—on a distraught older physician (O'Neill). The daughter (Louise) of the mishap's victim (Byington) is interested in Flynn, but then turns on him when she suspects him of being responsible for her mother's death. Fortunately, the surgical nurse on the case (Lindsay) tells the daughter the true story. In the meantime, Flynn has decided to risk his life in bacteriological experiments to find a vaccine for spotted fever. He survives the dreaded sickness, thereby proving his serum's effectiveness, and is reunited with the young lady. In the novel the leading character did not contract spotted fever.

Weaving in and out of this maze of noble self-sacrifice, as an observer of life's rich pageant, is a cathedral dean (Hardwicke) who pontificates profusely about the power of Altruism, Forgiveness, Faith, Science, Eternity, et al.

Lutheran minister turned novelist Lloyd C. Douglas *(The Robe)* wrote the 1935 inspirational best seller from which this painfully dated film was derived.

Flynn looks as though he tried hard to believe in it all, but occasionally his impish smile sneaks through. The box-office results proved that the mass audience, emerging from the Depression years, bought it all the way down the line.

With Walter Abel, Margaret Lindsay, Anita Louise, and Henry O'Neill

The Prince and the Pauper

With Bobby Mauch

1937   A First National Picture (Warner Bros.). Directed by William Keighley. Executive Producer: Hal B. Wallis. Associate Producer: Robert Lord. Screenplay by Laird Doyle. Dramatic version by Catherine Chisholm Cushing. Based on the novel by Mark Twain. Music by Erich Wolfgang Korngold. Director of Photography: Sol Polito. Film Editor: Ralph Dawson. Art Director: Robert Haas. Sound: Oliver S. Garretson. Gowns: Milo Anderson. Special Effects: Willard Van Enger and James Gibbons. Orchestrations: Hugo Friedhofer and Milan Roder. Assistant Director: Chuck Hansen. Running time: 120 minutes.

CAST

Miles Hendon	ERROL FLYNN
Earl of Hertford	Claude RAINS
Duke of Norfolk	Henry STEPHENSON
John Canty	Barton MacLANE
Tom Canty	Billy MAUCH
Prince Edward	Bobby MAUCH
Captain of the Guard	Alan HALE
First Lord	Eric Portman
Second Lord	Lionel Pape
Third Lord	Leonard Willey
Hugo	Murray Kinnell
Archbishop	Halliwell Hobbes
Barmaid	Phyllis Barry
Clemens	Ivan Simpson
Henry VIII	Montagu Love
Father Andrew	Fritz Leiber
Grandmother Canty	Elspeth Dudgeon
Mrs. Canty	Mary Field
Meaty Man	Forrester Harvey
Lady Jane Seymour	Helen Valkis
St. John	Lester Matthews
First Guard	Robert Adair
Second Guard	Harry Cording
Lord Warwick	Robert Warwick
Rich Man	Robert Evans
First Doctor	Holmes Herbert
Second Doctor	Ian MacLaren
Lady Jane Grey	Ann Howard
Lady Elizabeth	Gwendolyn Jones
Ruffler	Lionel Braham
The Watch	Harry Beresford
Innkeeper	Lionel Belmore
Proprietor	Ian Wolfe

St. Luke's Choristers

With Bobby Mauch, as the prince in the guise of the pauper

With Claude Rains and Billy Mauch, as the pauper in the guise of the prince

The Coronation, with Billy Mauch

With Billy Mauch, left, and on either side of Bobby Mauch, Henry Stephenson, and Robert Warwick

IN later years, Flynn played a supporting role to a young boy, Dean Stockwell, in *Kim*. In *The Prince and the Pauper* he plays second fiddle to twin boys, Billy and Bobby Mauch, who enact the look-alikes, Prince Edward (later King Edward VI) of England and a fictional beggar boy.

In this Mark Twain story the young prince, for a lark, changes clothes with Tom, the young pauper. The lark has repercussions when the real prince, mistaken for Tom, is driven away from the palace. The court assumes the other boy, despite his peculiar behavior, to be the prince, who is soon to be crowned king. The real prince is befriended by a soldier of fortune (Flynn), who takes the boy's frequent assertions of royal birth as a sign of madness.

On the morning of the coronation Edward eludes his protector and makes his way to Westminister Abbey, where he reveals who he is and forbids the ceremony. The hiding place of the Great Seal is made the final test of his claims; and, assisted by the Tom's suggestions, he reveals it and is crowned king.

Flynn had relatively little to do, and seemed to do even that with an air of casual indifference. His presence was merely a sop to the box office. He did have a short duel in the woods with Alan Hale, but it was not in the same league with his later classic encounters. Hale became a friend of Flynn's, and the two appeared in twelve pictures together. He was generally Flynn's humorous and rough-hewn sidekick, but in this, their first film together, they are enemies, and Hale is run through.

The Prince and the Pauper emerged as a handsomely proper piece without much excitement, but with compensating charm and gentle humor.

The real gimmick was the lengthy enactment of the coronation ceremony. Warners played this up, and released the picture just ahead of the much-heralded coronation of George VI, following Edward VIII's abdication. Another picture that made a point of including a coronation ceremony, *The Prisoner of Zenda*, was released just after the actual event.

The main theme of the score by Erich Korngold was reprised a decade later as the basis for the final movement of his Violin Concerto.

55

Another Dawn

With Kay Francis

1937 A Warner Brothers Picture. Directed by William Dieterle. Executive Producer: Hal B. Wallis. Associate Producer: Harry Joe Brown. Original Screenplay by Laird Doyle. Music by Erich Wolfgang Korngold. Director of Photography: Tony Gaudio. Dialogue Director: Stanley Logan. Film Editor: Ralph Dawson. Art Director: Robert Haas. Sound: Robert B. Lee. Gowns: Orry-Kelly. Special Effects: Willard Van Enger and James Gibbons. Orchestrations: Hugo Friedhofer and Milan Roder. Assistant Director: Frank Heath. Running time: 73 minutes.

CAST

Julia Ashton	KAY FRANCIS
Captain Denny Roark	ERROL FLYNN
Colonel Wister	Ian HUNTER
Grace Roark	Frieda INESCOURT
Wilkins	Herbert Mundin
Lord Alden	G. P. Huntley, Jr.
Hawkins	Billy Bevan
Sergeant Murphy	Clyde Cook
Henderson	Richard Powell
Sir Charles Benton	Kenneth Hunter
Mrs. Benton	Mary Forbes
Mrs. Farnold	Eily Malyon
Yeoman	Charles Austin
Butler	Joseph Tozer
Mr. Romkoff	Ben Welden
Fromby	Spencer Teakle
Campbell	David Clyde
Kelly	Charles Irwin
Wireless Operator	Reginald Sheffield
Ali	Martin Garralaga
Achaben	George Regas
Lang	Jack Richardson
Glass	Edward Dew
Lloyd	R. M. Simpson

Although Flynn played in various types of films other than swashbucklers, he did only two or three that could legitimately be called "soap operas." *Green Light* appeared early in 1937 and was followed a few months later by *Another Dawn,* both basically of the soap-opera school.

In this improbable love story, Flynn played a gentlemanly British army officer stationed at a remote outpost in the Sahara. He falls in love with the wife (Francis) of his commanding officer

(Hunter), and, because he reminds her of her great love who was killed in World War I, she responds to his feeling. But the triangle is one of honor, and the participants behave with decency and decorum. There are numerous sequences in which the discussion centers about the merits of ethical and unethical love. The magnanimous and understanding Hunter eventually flies off on a suicide mission in order to undo a military blunder, leaving the lovers to their destiny and "another dawn."

The only excitement in the film is a mild and unconvincing skirmish with Arabs in the desert, and a sandstorm.

Tedious and terribly dated, the picture does have a certain faded charm and presents a twenty-eight-year-old Flynn as the kind of beautifully spoken, old school tie, cricket- and polo-playing Briton so fashionable in Hollywood in those halcyon days before the sun set on the British Empire.

The romance, in part, echoes the triangle and final sacrifice of one of the lovers in *The Charge of the Light Brigade,* with Flynn reversing roles. The desert outpost also was reminiscent of *The Charge;* indeed, it was basically the same set, redressed.

Korngold composed a beautiful score—considerably beyond the demands of the film—and thought so well of his major theme that he made excellent use of it in the Violin Concerto he wrote for Jascha Heifetz years later.

With Kay Francis

With Ian Hunter

With Herbert Mundin and Billy Bevan

The Perfect Specimen

With Joan Blondell

1937 A First National Picture (Warner Bros.). Directed by Michael Curtiz. Executive Producer: Hal B. Wallis. Associate Producer: Harry Joe Brown. Screenplay by Norman Reilly Raine, Lawrence Riley, Brewster Morse, and Fritz Falkenstein. Based on the *Cosmopolitan* magazine story by Samuel Hopkins Adams. Music by Heinz Roemheld. Director of Photography: Charles Rosher. Dialogue Director: Gene Lewis. Film Editor: Terry Morse. Art Director: Robert Haas. Sound: Everett A. Brown. Gowns: Howard Shoup. Special Effects: Byron Haskin, Edwin DuPar, and Rex Wimpy. Assistant Director: Frank Heath. Running time: 97 minutes.

CAST
Gerald Beresford Wicks	ERROL FLYNN
Mona Carter	JOAN BLONDELL
Killigrew Shaw	Hugh Herbert
Mr. Grattan	Edward Everett Horton
Jink Carter	Dick Foran
Alicia	Beverly Roberts
Mrs. Leona Wicks	May Robson
Pinky	Allen Jenkins
Clarabelle	Dennie Moore
Hotel Clerk	Hugh O'Connell
Snodgrass	James Burke
Hooker	Granville Bates
Carl Carter	Harry Davenport
Briggs	Tim Henning
Station Master	Spencer Charters

THIS was Flynn's comedy debut, and it also allowed him to display his natural endowments. Since Flynn appeared to be a fine specimen—handsome, intelligent, charming, cultured, and athletic, it seemed reasonable to cast him in a role that was an exaggeration of all these qualities.

The Perfect Specimen, based on a story by Samuel Hopkins Adams, was reminiscent in some ways of the same author's *It Happened One Night.* Flynn was the model son and heir of a wealthy, upper-class family who was reared and cultivated by his tyrannical aunt (Robson) in the manner of a hothouse plant. Never outside the gates of his estate, he had been dedicated since childhood to a rigorous program designed towards the perfection of the ultimate man. What he lacks are humility and rapport with his fellow humans, and these qualities are supplied primarily by contact with a newspaper reporter (Blondell), who crashes her car through the estate's fence while the Perfect Specimen is testing a Newtonian theory by falling out of a tree. Her curiosity and interest lure him to the outside world, where he proves himself capable of hurdling the pitfalls of

With Edward Everett Horton, May Robson and Joan Blondell

runner to his *Gentleman Jim* five years later—and it was apparent that the actor had genuine form and style as a boxer.

Warners' publicity department let a story circulate saying that Flynn had represented Australia as a boxer in the 1928 Olympics at Amsterdam. Not until many years later did Flynn deny the story as completely false.

With Joan Blondell and Hugh Herbert

his newly discovered emancipation, and, at the same time, manages to fall in love with Blondell.

Despite swift pacing and a good cast, the script was a little complicated and arch, and Flynn was not yet sufficiently in command as a film actor to do the part full credit. In one sequence he was allowed to perform in the boxing ring—a fore-

The Adventures of Robin Hood

1938 A First National Picture (Warner Bros.). Technicolor. Directed by Michael Curtiz and William Keighley. Executive Producer: Hal B. Wallis. Associate Producer: Henry Blanke. Original Screenplay by Norman Reilly Raine and Seton I. Miller. Based upon ancient Robin Hood legends. Music by Erich Wolfgang Korngold. Directors of Photography: Sol Polito and Tony Gaudio. Associate Technicolor Photographer: W. Howard Greene. Dialogue Director: Irving Rapper. Film Editor: Ralph Dawson. Art Director: Carl Jules Weyl. Costumes by Milo Anderson. Make-up Artist: Perc Westmore. Sound Recorder: C. A. Riggs. Orchestrations: Hugo Friedhofer and Milan Roder. Assistant Directors: Lee Katz and Jack Sullivan. Technical Adviser: Louis Van Den Ecker. Archery Supervisor: Howard Hill. Fencing Master: Fred Cavens. Technicolor Color Director: Natalie Kalmus. Technicolor Color Consultant: Morgan Padelford. Unit Production Manager: Al Alleborn. Contributor to screenplay treatment: Rowland Leigh. Running time: 102 minutes.

CAST

Sir Robin of Locksley (Robin Hood)	ERROL FLYNN
Maid Marian	Olivia de HAVILLAND
Sir Guy of Gisbourne	Basil RATHBONE
Prince John	Claude RAINS
Will Scarlet	Patric Knowles
Friar Tuck	Eugene Pallette
Little John	Alan Hale
High Sheriff of Nottingham	Melville Cooper
King Richard	Ian Hunter
Bess	Una O'Connor
Much the Miller's Son	Herbert Mundin
Bishop of Black Canons	Montagu Love
Sir Essex	Leonard Willey
Sir Ralf	Robert Noble
Sir Mortimer	Kenneth Hunter
Sir Geoffrey	Robert Warwick
Sir Baldwin	Colin Kenny
Sir Ivor	Lester Matthews
Dickon Malbete	Harry Cording
Captain of Archers	Howard Hill
Properietor of Kent Road Tavern	Ivan Simpson

60

*Far left—Harry Cording. Basil Rath-
bone in foreground*

61

WARNER BROTHERS first considered filming *Robin Hood* in 1935 with James Cagney slated for the title role and contract player Guy Kibbee as Friar Tuck. But in November of that year Cagney walked off the lot for a lengthy dispute, and one month later Flynn's *Captain Blood* was released. After that film's extraordinary impact, *Robin Hood* was tailored for Flynn and given a budget of $1,600,000—the largest sum allotted to a Warner film up to that time. (The cost eventually reached $2 million.)

The screenplay is considerably different from that of Douglas Fairbanks' 1922 silent epic. Fairbanks chose to do an original treatment that made use of virtually none of the material in the ballads, legends, or later stories. Since his version was copyrighted, Warners could not use any of Fairbanks' ideas or situations.

The Warner approach drew from all other sources, though. Sir Robin of Locksley is presented as a Saxon knight incensed at the evil doings of Prince John (Rains) and the Norman barons while King Richard the Lion-Hearted (Hunter) is being held for ransom in Austria after his departure from the Third Crusade in Palestine. The heavy emphasis on the oppressive treatment of the Saxons by the Norman knights (which some scholars say didn't exist as late as the end of the twelfth century) was taken from Sir Walter Scott's novel *Ivanhoe*.

Robin becomes an outlaw with his band of followers, and they headquarter in Sherwood Forest near the town of Nottingham, doing everything possible to aid the poor Saxons and to thwart Prince John and his minions. One marvelous scene has them swinging, dropping, and diving from the oaks and sycamores onto a Norman party on horseback.

With Alan Hale and Eugene Pallette

With Alan Hale and director William Keighley, beneath camera

With Eugene Pallette

With Olivia de Havilland

Some of the favorite incidents of the Robin Hood legend were used on the screen for the first time: the bout with quarterstaves between Robin and Little John on a log spanning a stream (Alan Hale played Little John in both the Fairbanks and Flynn versions, as well as in a 1950 film, *Rogues of Sherwood Forest*), Robin's first meeting with Friar Tuck (Pallette), and his forcing the rotund cleric to carry him piggyback across the stream. All the various archery contests described in the many versions were amalgamated into one major Archery Tournament, wherein Robin splits his opponent's arrow (actually accomplished by archery champion Howard Hill) and wins the Golden Arrow prize.

Robin and Sir Guy of Gisbourne (Rathbone),

With Melville Cooper, Basil Rathbone, Olivia de Havilland, and Claude Rains

chief conspirer under Prince John, become rivals for Lady Marian (de Havilland), a Norman ward of Richard's. This triangle, not present in any of the old ballads, originated in the De Koven-Smith light opera version of *Robin Hood* in 1890.

After Marian helps Robin's band free him from the hangman's noose, it is evident that they are in love. Prince John imprisons her in Nottingham Castle for treason and prepares to be crowned

63

king, having officially declared the absent Richard dead. But Richard and a small retinue dressed in monk's habit have secretly returned to England and are in Sherwood to seek out Robin (an incident from the old ballads). Robin's entire band and Richard—all disguised as monks—enter Nottingham Castle and disrupt the coronation ceremony (echoes of the coronation of George VI and the Warner-Flynn *Prince and the Pauper*). After a magnificent battle royal, Marian is rescued, John is ousted, and Richard reigns again.

Since there was a little something, at least, from all sources, Flynn was required to engage in some lithe leaping, wall-scaling, vaulting, and vine-swinging to take into account the Fairbanks heritage.

In September, 1937, the cast and crew, under the guidance of director William Keighley, traveled approximately five hundred milles to Bidwell Park in the town of Chico, California, to film the Sherwood Forest sequences. B. Reeves (Breezy) Eason directed some of the second-unit material involving horse action at the same location. Eason originally was engaged to direct portions of a major jousting sequence which was to open the picture. This episode was eliminated during production, and, as far as can be determined, nothing was ever shot for it.

After the company returned from Chico in November, shooting started on the Archery Tournament at the old Busch Gardens in Pasadena, but, as producer Henry Blanke recalls, it was soon decided by Jack Warner, Hal Wallis and Blanke to replace Keighley with Michael Curtiz. The reasons seemed to have been Keighley's too light-hearted approach to the material and the lack of impact in his action sequences.

Curtiz directed all of the interiors as well as additional scenes (possibly with Eason) near Lake Sherwood, just west of the San Fernando Valley, in order to embellish and punch up the action sequences previously done at Chico.

In his autobiography, Flynn took pride in the fact that in this picture he did most of his own stunts and dueling. The final duel took place in Nottingham Castle, where Robin and Sir Guy covered a considerable area during the course of the action. Curtiz loved to use scenery, props, and lighting effects to increase the theatricalism of his duels, and in *Robin Hood* hero and villain fought their way down a winding staircase, upset a giant candelabra, locked blades over a heavy table, slashed candles, etc. Huge shadows of the two figures on a pillar as they came together in a *corps-a-corps* were photographed to good effect. Occasionally the opponents would pause during

64

With Olivia de Havilland

the clash of steel long enough to spout such exchanges of dialogue as:

Robin: Did I upset your plans?
Sir Guy: You've come to Nottingham once too
often!
Robin: When this is over, my friend, there'll
be no need for me to come again!

Broadswords were used, but liberties were taken with the techniques. Actual medieval swords were heavy, hacking weapons and were handled in a primitive fashion. In *Robin Hood* fencing techniques that were not developed until centuries later (*e.g.,* the lunge, certain parries) were incorporated into the routine.

Flynn looked first-rate with a sword, and had overcome some of the awkwardness he evidenced in *Captain Blood*. Rathbone was superb. He had become genuinely interested in fencing since *Captain Blood,* and took many lessons from the fencing master and stager of screen duels, Fred Cavens. Flynn, on the other hand, had neither the

With Basil Rathbone

With Basil Rathbone

discipline nor the interest for constant practice. Fortunately he was a natural athlete, and his form and flair made his dueling look good on the screen.

Erich Wolfgang Korngold's masterful score considerably aided the duel. Rich with brass and percussive effects, the thick-textured strains emphasized each stroke of the blades. The entire

With Basil Rathbone

score remains one of the most perfect blends of film and music.

In addition to all the other ingredients, Warners used the then new three-color Technicolor process. It was a wise decision, as the legendary subject with its many forest scenes, costumes and pageantry, was perfect for full color. The lush greens and russets of Sherwood and the cool tones of Nottingham Castle were esthetically pleasing. Seen today, the color is still extraordinary and one of the best examples of the old three-strip Technicolor process which has been obsolete since the mid-1950s.

Although action was the keynote of *The Adventures of Robin Hood,* there also was above-average dialogue, spirited performances, and impressive spectacle. Said Frank Nugent in *The New York Times:* "Life and the movies have their compensations, and such a film as this is payment in full for many dull hours of picture-going. A richly produced, bravely bedecked, romantic and color-ful show, it leaps boldly to the forefront of this year's best and can be calculated to rejoice the eights, rejuvenate the eighties, and delight those in between."

Almost all critics and audiences echoed the above; the picture was a huge success, and to this day remains a fine film. Certainly it is the one vehicle above all others by which Flynn will be remembered. His playing was by turns virile, jocular, determined, athletic, tender, and romantic. His quiet and yet intense love scenes with Olivia de Havilland are the best the two had in their many pictures together.

A sequel, *Sir Robin of Locksley,* was announced by Warners but never developed. In 1948 *The Adventures of Robin Hood* was given a full-scale national reissue with new Technicolor prints, and did far better than average business. The picture was re-released again—but in black and white only, and on a more limited basis—just before being sold to television in the mid-1950s.

With Olivia de Havilland, Ian Hunter, Eugene Pallette, Alan Hale, Herbert Mundin, and Patric Knowles

With Walter Connolly, Olivia de Havilland, and Rosalind Russell

With Patric Knowles

Four's a Crowd

1938 A Warner Brothers Picture. Directed by Michael Curtiz. Executive Producer: Hal B. Wallis. Associate Producer: David Lewis. Screenplay by Casey Robinson and Sig Herzig. Based on an original story by Wallace Sullivan. Music by Heinz Roemheld and Ray Heindorf. Director of Photography: Ernest Haller. Dialogue Director: Irving Rapper. Film Editor: Clarence Kolster. Art Director: Max Parker. Sound: Robert B. Lee. Gowns: Orry-Kelly. Assistant Director: Sherry Shourds. Running time: 91 minutes.

CAST *Robert Kensington Lansford*
ERROL FLYNN

Lorri Dillingwell	OLIVIA de HAVILLAND
Jean Christy	ROSALIND RUSSELL
Patterson Buckley	PATRIC KNOWLES
John P. Dillingwell	Walter Connolly
Silas Jenkins	Hugh Herbert
Bingham	Melville Cooper
Preston	Franklin Pangborn
Herman (Barber)	Herman Bing
Amy	Margaret Hamilton
Butler Pierce	Joseph Crehan
Young	Joe Cunningham
Buckley's Secretary	Dennie Moore
Lansford's 1st Secretary	Gloria Blondell
Lansford's 2nd Secretary	Carole Landis
Mrs. Jenkins	Reine Riano
Dr. Ives	Charles Trowbridge
Charlie	Spencer Charters

With Rosalind Russell

As a change of pace from *Robin Hood,* Flynn was immediately put into a modern, fast-moving farce along the lines of the very popular so-called "screwball comedy" cycle of the day.

Although the diffused, slapstick material and approach have lost their appeal, Flynn holds up surprisingly well as a light comedian, performing in an early Cary Grant manner. He handled himself with much more assurance than in his one previous comedic effort, *The Perfect Specimen,* and was less coy and cute than in his later *Footsteps in the Dark* and *Never Say Goodbye.*

In *Four's a Crowd* he played an expert public relations man, a promoter who takes on the job of eulogizing a mean-spirited, crotchety millionaire (Connolly). As a means to this end, Flynn goes back to his previous job as managing editor of a newspaper owned by Patric Knowles. While working on Connolly, he makes love to his daughter (de Havilland) and a reporter (Russell), but the foursome headed for the altar at the film's ending are Flynn and Russell and Knowles and de Havilland.

Flynn was a humorous and sometimes witty man. With these qualities, combined with his charm and impishness, it's possible he may have become an accomplished light comedian with the right script and good direction. But the public was only mildly responsive to this aspect of his talent.

With Olivia de Havilland, Patric Knowles, Hugh Herbert, and Rosalind Russell

The Sisters

1938   A Warner Brothers Picture. Directed by Anatole Litvak. Executive Producer: Hal B. Wallis. Associate Producer: David Lewis. Screenplay by Milton Krims. Based on the novel by Myron Brinig. Music by Max Steiner. Director of Photography: Tony Gaudio. Dialogue Director: Irving Rapper. Film Editor: Warren Low. Art Director: Carl Jules Weyl. Sound: C. A. Riggs. Gowns: Orry-Kelly. Orchestrations: Hugo Friedhofer. Assistant Director: Jack Sullivan. Running time: 99 minutes.

CAST		
Frank Medlin	ERROL FLYNN
Louise Elliott	BETTE DAVIS
Helen Elliott	Anita Louise
William Benson	Ian Hunter
Tim Hazelton	Donald Crisp
Rose Elliott	Beulah Bondi
Grace Elliott	Jane Bryan
Sam Johnson	Alan Hale
Tom Knivel	Dick Foran
Ned Elliott	Henry Travers
Norman French	Patric Knowles
Flora Gibbon	Lee Patrick
Flora's Mother	Laura Hope Crews
Stella Johnson	Janet Shaw
Doc Moore	Harry Davenport
Laura Bennett	Ruth Garland
Anthony Bittick	John Warburton
Caleb Ammon	Paul Harvey
Blonde	Mayo Methot
Robert Forbes	Irving Bacon
Tom Selig	Arthur Hoyt
Ship's Captain	Stanley Fields
Telephone Operator	Susan Hayward

BY focusing on three daughters of a small-town druggist in Montana who fall in love and marry widely different types of men, Myron Brinig's 1937 best-selling novel presented a panorama of American life just after the turn of the century. The film concentrated more on one sister (Davis) and her trials with a young San Francisco newspaperman (Flynn), whom she marries.

This was Flynn's first opportunity, since becoming a star, to play something other than a reputable leading man. In *The Sisters* he was required to portray a weak, unstable, immature charmer with a penchant for alcohol. Despite some writing ability and his understanding and sacrificing wife, he cannot make a success of himself, and eventually, because of his shame, the desire to escape, and the hope of coming to grips with himself, he ships out for Singapore.

Under Anatole Litvak's direction, Flynn performed creditably; but, in playing a weakling, he did not yet possess quite enough ability and range to fully overcome his own winning personality and appearance.

The Sisters was essentially a Bette Davis picture, although Flynn insisted on top billing. Davis performed beautifully in this handsomely

71

With Bette Davis

mounted, well-directed, and sincere adaptation, which included a short, but effective, re-creation of the 1906 San Francisco earthquake and fire. This sequence was not nearly as long nor as spectacular as the climax to MGM's *San Francisco* two years earlier, but it was not meant to be the highlight or exploitable aspect of the production. For the earthquake montage, some stock footage from Warners' *Old San Francisco* (1927) was exhumed.

The final scenes were shot two ways: One, true to the novel, wherein Davis marries her erstwhile employer (Hunter), the other, a reconciliation between Davis and Flynn. After gauging preview audience reactions to both finales, Warners decided to release the latter version despite Flynn's protests.

In later years Flynn was to complain that Warners did not give him scope as an actor and that he constantly was forced into heroics. Actually, he was given a considerable variety of parts (though not always good parts nor in fine films), but it became apparent that the Flynn the public most wanted to see was the dashing hero. Naturally, reacting to consumer demand, Warners stressed the big action dramas more frequently than not.

With Ian Hunter and Donald Crisp

With David Niven

The Dawn Patrol

1938 A Warner Brothers Picture. Directed by Edmund Goulding. Executive Producer: Hal B. Wallis. Associate Producer: Robert Lord. Screenplay by Seton I. Miller and Dan Totheroh. Based on an original story, "Flight Commander," by John Monk Saunders and Howard Hawks. Music by Max Steiner. Director of Photography: Tony Gaudio. Film Editor: Ralph Dawson. Art Director: John Hughes. Sound: C. A. Riggs. Special Effects: Edwin A. DuPar. Orchestrations: Hugo Friedhofer. Assistant Director: Frank Heath. Technical Adviser: Captain L. G. S. Scott. Running time: 103 minutes.

CAST

Captain Courtney	ERROL FLYNN
Major Brand	Basil RATHBONE
Lieutenant Scott	David NIVEN
Phipps	Donald CRISP
Sergeant Watkins	Melville Cooper
Bott	Barry Fitzgerald
Von Mueller	Carl Esmond
Hollister	Peter Willes
Ronnie	Morton Lowry
Squires	Michael Brooke
Flaherty	James Burke
Bentham	Stuart Hall
Scott's Mechanic	Herbert Evans
Major Brand's Orderly	Sidney Bracy

With Basil Rathbone

THE original version of *The Dawn Patrol* was produced in 1930 during the big World War I aviation cycle that included *Wings* and *Hell's Angels*. Eight years later Warners decided to remake it with an all-British cast headed by Flynn, Basil Rathbone, and David Niven in the roles originally played by Richard Barthelmess, Neil Hamilton, and Douglas Fairbanks, Jr.

Every sequence followed the earlier Howard Hawks version very closely, except for the dialogue, which was revised by Seton I. Miller and director Edmund Goulding.

The Dawn Patrol tells a story about the 59th Squadron of the British Royal Flying Corps in France at a time during World War I when German aircraft was driving the British back. Using

With David Niven and Michael Brooke

With David Niven and James Burke. In the background: Donald Crisp, Melville Cooper, Carl Esmond, and Michael Brooke

obsolete planes and equipment, the Royal Flying Corps valiantly tries to buck the onslaught. The squadron commander's (Rathbone) sole satisfaction, upon being promoted, is to turn his old nerve-wracking job over to air ace Courtney (Flynn), who has called him a butcher. Before long the anguish of such a command makes Courtney lose control of his nerves and take to the bottle. After he sends flyer Scott's (Niven) younger brother to his death on his first patrol, Courtney's relationship with his good friend is shattered, and to make retribution, he takes a suicidal assignment for which Scott had volunteered (bombing an ammunition dump behind enemy lines). In the course of it he engages in an air duel with von Richter, the feared German ace, and later is shot down

and killed. The picture ends with Scott taking over the thankless job of squadron commander.

All the flying footage from the first version was used again in the new one, including the bombing of the ammo depot done in miniature. In place of the original principals' closeups in the air, well-integrated process shots were made. The dogfights and a raid by Courtney and Scott on von Richter's squadron headquarters had style and excitement, although they were not as spectacular in terms of number of planes in the air as in *Hell's Angels*.

Many scenes are situated in the club bar of the flyers' headquarters, where the names of downed airmen are constantly erased from the blackboard and "Poor Butterfly" is played repeatedly on a small gramophone. Brandy, whiskey, and soda flow; an air of doomed comraderie prevails. In the next room, Major Brand, the pressure overwhelming, blurts out: "It's a slaughter house, that's what it is, and I'm the executioner. You send men in rotten ships up to die. . . . They don't argue or revolt. . . . They just say 'Righto' and go out and do it."

At the bar the flyers sing:

So stand by your glasses steady,
This world is a world of lies.
Here's to the dead already—
Hurrah for the next man who dies!

And Brand reacts: "Listen to them. Bluffing themselves, pretending death doesn't mean anything to them, trying to live just for the minute—the hour, pretending they don't care if they go up tomorrow and never come back."

Warners went to their Calabasas Ranch for the exterior airfield shots. Resurrected Nieuports (the most widely used Allied fighter) were augmented with Thomas-Morse Scouts, and the resulting combination of authentic and doctored aircraft, quantity vintage footage, and carefully matched new material was superb.

Flynn and Niven had more charm and better chemistry going for them than Barthelmess and Fairbanks. They played extremely well together, both in the light-hearted early scenes where daredeviltry, lack of discipline, and undergraduate humor were predominant, and in the grim, tense later scenes of sheer helplessness and futility. Flynn received excellent reviews, as did all of the performers and the film in general. It remains one

With Donald Crisp, Morton Lowry, and David Niven

of Flynn's better pictures, and one of the best World War I aviation films.

The Dawn Patrol's pacifistic overtones were heard just a few months before the beginning of World War II. While the film may have been a grim reminder flavored with nostalgia to the old veterans, to the young and uninitiated only the guts and the glory stood out.

Dodge City

With Olivia de Havilland and Ann Sheridan

1939   A Warner Brothers Picture. Technicolor. Directed by Michael Curtiz. Executive Producer: Hal B. Wallis. Associate Producer: Robert Lord. Original Screenplay by Robert Buckner. Music by Max Steiner. Director of Photography: Sol Polito. Associate Technicolor Photographer: Ray Rennahan. Dialogue Director: Jo Graham. Film Editor: George Amy. Art Director: Ted Smith. Sound: Oliver S. Garretson. Costumes: Milo Anderson. Makeup: Perc Westmore. Special Effects: Byron Haskin and Rex Wimpy. Orchestrations: Hugo Friedhofer. Assistant Director: Sherry Shourds. Color Consultant: Morgan Padelford. Runnnig time: 104 minutes.

With Guinn (Big Boy) Williams

CAST

Wade Hatton	ERROL FLYNN	*Mrs. Cole*	Gloria Holden
Abbie Irving	Olivia de HAVILLAND	*Munger*	Douglas Fowley
Ruby Gilman	Ann SHERIDAN	*Mrs. Irving*	Georgia Caine
Jeff Surrett	Bruce Cabot	*Surrett's Lawyer*	Charles Halton
Joe Clemens	Frank McHugh	*Bud Taylor*	Ward Bond
Rusty Hart	Alan Hale	*Mrs. McCoy*	Cora Witherspoon
Matt Cole	John Litel	*Orth*	Russell Simpson
Dr. Irving	Henry Travers	*Barlow*	Monte Blue
Colonel Dodge	Henry O'Neill	*Crocker*	Nat Carr
Yancey	Victor Jory	*Barber*	Clem Bevans
Lee Irving	William Lundigan	*Hammond*	Joseph Crehan
Tex Baird	Guinn (Big Boy) Williams	*Twitchell*	Thurston Hall
Harry Cole	Bobs Watson	*Coggins*	Chester Clute

With Chester Clute, Henry O'Neill, Thurston Hall,
Joseph Crehan, Alan Hale, and Guinn (Big Boy) Williams

*With Olivia de Havilland and
Henry Travers*

THE year 1939 could go down in film history as the year of the big Western. A genre during the early thirties that had been for the most part restricted to B pictures and serials, it suddenly was reintroduced on a large scale with the success of *The Plainsman* (1936) and *Wells Fargo* (1937).

During 1939 such films as *Stagecoach, Destry Rides Again, Union Pacific, Jesse James,* and *Man of Conquest* were given big budgets and lots of exploitation. *The Oklahoma Kid* with Cagney and *Dodge City* with Flynn were Warners' two entries, but the latter had Technicolor and a much more lavish production.

Dodge City contained generous servings of large-scale Western ingredients: A wide-open frontier town in need of a cleanup, a definitive saloon brawl, wagon trains, the prairie with its roving herds of buffalo, cowboys driving their long-horned cattle along the Chisholm Trail, a race between train and stagecoach, gun fights, a cattle stampede, an attempted lynching—all captured with Michael Curtiz' eye for hell-for-leather action and pictorial sweep.

The saloon brawl remains a model for a mass slugfest. The breadth and vigor of the staging and stunt work (including two cowboys crashing

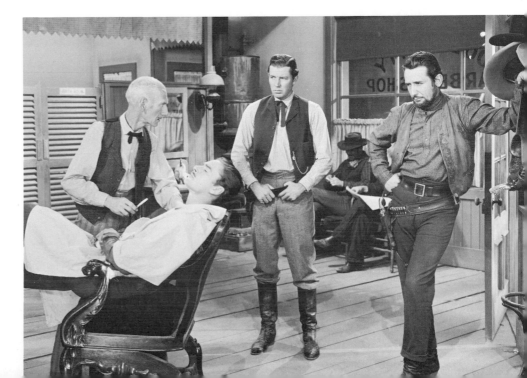

*With Clem Bevans, Bruce Cabot,
and Victor Jory*

With Bruce Cabot, Victor Jory, and Douglas Fowley

through a staircase to the floor from a balcony) were all one could ask for.

Flynn was cast in the rather incongruous role of an Irish soldier of fortune transplanted to the West who turns sheriff, and in due course brings law and order to the mushrooming cattle town of Dodge City. To offset any amazement that a man with a cultured British accent, with imposed Irish flavoring, should be galloping around the Wild West, care was taken to have other characters near the beginning of the film discuss the "Irishman who had been everywhere and done everything. First, he was in India with the British Army, a revolution in Cuba, punching cattle in Texas before he fought for the rebels in 'Jeb' Stuart's cavalry." After audiences accepted Flynn wholeheartedly in *Dodge City,* the studio never bothered to rationalize his British speech and manners in subsequent Westerns.

The exteriors were photographed at the Warner

Ranch in Calabasas and near Modesto, California.

Dodge City's only flaw was the lack of a superior script. The locales and action sequences taken individually were impressive, but the writing and characters were elementary and stereotyped. In 1939, the "adult" or "psychological" Western was still embryonic, and *Dodge City,* except for its production values, cast, and range of ingredients, was really standard, uncomplicated good guys versus bad guys.

This was the first of eight Westerns Flynn made over an eleven-year period. They ranged from good to mediocre; but a Technicolor print of *Dodge City* combined with *They Died with Their Boots On*—despite their faults—would be the two most representative and generally enjoyable examples of his work in this genre for retrospective purposes.

In 1951 Warners reissued *Dodge City* (in a black-and-white print), coupled with *Virginia City,* in line with a current Civil War Western film cycle. The two films did exceptionally well.

With Olivia de Havilland and Alan Hale

With Olivia de Havilland

81

The Private Lives of Elizabeth and Essex

With Bette Davis

1939 A Warner Brothers-First National Picture. Technicolor. Directed by Michael Curtiz. Executive Producer: Hal B. Wallis. Associate Producer: Robert Lord. Screenplay by Norman Reilly Raine and Aeneas MacKenzie. Based on the play *Elizabeth the Queen* by Maxwell Anderson. Music by Erich Wolfgang Korngold. Director of Photography: Sol Polito. Associate Technicolor Photographer: W. Howard Greene. Dialogue Director: Stanley Logan. Film Editor: Owen Marks. Art Director: Anton Grot. Sound: C. A. Riggs. Costumes: Orry-Kelly. Make-up: Perc Westmore. Special Effects: Byron Haskin and H. F. Koenekamp. Orchestrations: Hugo Friedhofer and Milan Roder. Assistant Director: Sherry Shourds. Technical Adviser: Ali Hubert. Color Consultant: Morgan Padelford. Unit Manager: Frank Mattison. Running time: 106 minutes.

CAST
Queen Elizabeth	BETTE DAVIS
Earl of Essex	ERROL FLYNN
Lady Penelope Gray	
	Olivia de HAVILLAND
Francis Bacon	Donald Crisp
Earl of Tyrone	Alan Hale
Sir Walter Raleigh	Vincent Price
Lord Burghley	Henry Stephenson
Sir Robert Cecil	Henry Daniell
Sir Thomas Egerton	James Stephenson

Mistress Margaret Radcliffe	
	Nanette Fabares*
Lord Knollys	Ralph Forbes
Lord Mountjoy	Robert Warwick
Sir Edward Coke	Leo G. Carroll

*later known as Nanette Fabray

AT the time of *Elizabeth and Essex* Errol Flynn had risen to be one of the biggest box-office stars in America. But Bette Davis was undoubt-

With Bette Davis

83

With Vincent Price and Donald Crisp

With James Stephenson and Robert Warwick

With Olivia de Havilland

edly the queen of Warners. The two were completely dissimilar in attitude and temperament: the shrewd, perfectionistic, hard-driving Davis and the charming, impetuous, fun-loving Flynn. They did not get along at all. At the time of *The Sisters,* the year before, Flynn had demanded and received top billing over Davis. At the start of their second film he insisted that the original title, *Elizabeth the Queen,* be changed to take into account his presence. When *The Knight and the Lady* was decided upon, Davis threatened to walk off the picture. *Elizabeth and Essex* was more to everyone's satisfaction, but Lytton Strachey had a book copyrighted with that title. Hence, *The Private Lives of Elizabeth and Essex.*

Davis was delighted with the prospect of portraying Elizabeth, the dominating and courageous queen of England and daughter of Henry VIII. But she had asked that Laurence Olivier be given the role of Essex. Warners assigned Flynn, and both stars were unhappy with their fates.

With Davis the unhappiness did not register in her performance, but with Flynn the enterprice was considerably less than satisfactory. He appeared either uncomfortable, nonchalant, or blithely boyish in many of his scenes with Davis, thus robbing the film of a good deal of credibility.

Handsomely mounted and beautifully photographed, *Elizabeth and Essex* is an adaptation of the 1930 Maxwell Anderson play written in alternate scenes of blank verse and poetic prose. It offers an imaginative interpretation of historical

84

With Donald Crisp

facts surrounding the relationship of two head-strong characters who profess love for one another but constantly clash in their personalities and ambitions.

As presented in the film, the middle-aged Elizabeth loves the youthful, power-hungry Essex, and at one point there is talk of marriage. But Essex wants to be king, not merely consort. When Elizabeth decides it is in the best interests of England to thwart his ambitions, she sentences him to death for treason, though she still loves him. Even as she entreats him to ask her parden, he goes off to die, for Essex realizes that inevitably he would play once more for power—almost in spite of himself—and he now knows the queen's peaceful policy is more beneficial than his warlike one.

With Bette Davis

85

Whereas all of the scenes in the play took place in the palace, the film opened up the staging to include a montage of the Cadiz battle, and went on to Essex's triumphal return to London (which was later lifted almost *en bloc* for *Adventures of Don Juan),* a scene on the grounds of Essex's country estate, the Irish marsh (re-created on a sound stage) for the sequence in which Essex is defeated by the Irish rebel, Tyrone (Hale), a dungeon in the Tower of London, and the execution block in the courtyard. The last scene was cut from the film after the initial release, presumably because of negative audience reaction.

Korngold's score was a splendid added dimension. Its heraldic brass passages and a poignant love theme were perfection for historical romance.

Flynn's usual co-star, Olivia de Havilland, was reduced to the supporting role of lady-in-waiting to the queen. She has an unrequited love for Essex, and even participates in a scheme to divide him and Elizabeth. Ironically, in only four of their eight pictures together do Errol and Olivia presumably live happily ever after: *Captain Blood, Robin Hood, Dodge City,* and *Santa Fe Trail.*

An interesting sidelight regarding the bitter blending of Flynn and Davis occurred in 1938, after completion of *The Sisters*. Warners offered independent producer David O. Selznick full financing for his *Gone with the Wind* and 25 per cent of the profits if he would use Flynn and Davis as Rhett and Scarlett in addition to de Havilland as Melanie. According to Davis and Jack L. Warner, Davis refused to have any part of a package deal involving Flynn, although she had always craved the role.

With Miriam Hopkins

Virginia City

1940   A Warner Brothers-First National Picture. Directed by Michael Curtiz. Executive Producer: Hal B. Wallis. Associate Producer: Robert Fellows. Original Screenplay by Robert Buckner. Music by Max Steiner. Director of Photography: Sol Polito. Dialogue Director: Jo Graham. Film Editor: George Amy. Art Director: Ted Smith. Sound: Oliver S. Garretson and Francis J. Scheid. Make-up: Perc Westmore. Special Effects: Byron Haskin and H. F. Koenekamp. Orchestrations: Hugo Friedhofer. Assistant Director: Sherry Shourds. Unit Manager: Frank Mattison. Running time: 121 minutes.

With Guinn (Big Boy) Williams, Humphrey Bogart, and Alan Hale.

With Alan Hale and Guinn (Big Boy) Williams

With Randolph Scott and Miriam Hopkins

CAST		
Kerry Bradford	ERROL FLYNN
Julia Hayne	MIRIAM HOPKINS
Vance Irby	Randolph SCOTT
John Murrell	Humphrey BOGART
Mr. Upjohn	Frank McHugh
Moose	Alan Hale
Marblehead	Guinn (Big Boy) Williams
Marshall	John Litel
Major Drewery	Douglass Dumbrille
Dr. Cameron	Moroni Olsen
Armistead	Russell Hicks
Cobby	Dickie Jones
Union Soldier	Frank Wilcox
Gaylord	Russell Simpson
Abraham Lincoln	Victor Kilian
Jefferson Davis	Charles Middleton
Stage Driver	Monte Montague
Murrell's Henchmen	{ George Regas
	{ Paul Fix
General Meade	Thurston Hall
Seddon	Charles Trowbridge
General Page	Howard Hickman
Ralston	Charles Halton
Sergeant	Ward Bond
Sam	Sam McDaniel
Scarecrow	Harry Cording
Fanatic	Trevor Bardette
Spieler	Tom Dugan
Bartender	Spencer Charters
Telegrapher	George Reeves

With Miriam Hopkins

AT the conclusion of *Dodge City*, Henry O'Neill as Colonel Dodge asks Flynn and his cohorts, Alan Hale and "Big Boy" Williams, to go on to Virginia City, another wide-open frontier town in dire need of a tamer the likes of Flynn. Realizing she cannot hold her man long in a sedate existence, Olivia de Havilland, good scout that she is, gives her sanction, and the fade-out leads everyone to believe that the door was being left open for a super-sequel.

Virginia City appeared one year later, but a sequel it isn't. The time is during rather than after the Civil War, and the characters bear different names. Olivia, along with Technicolor, is unfortunately missing.

Warners must have shared with others the concern for a better plotted script than the one for *Dodge City*; for both Norman Reilly Raine *(Robin Hood)* and Howard Koch *(Sea Hawk)* were uncredited contributors to the treatment and story construction of *Virginia City*. But, alas, although the final shooting script tells a good story, it abounds in unmercifully wooden scenes and dialogue.

Flynn plays a Union officer who escapes from the Confederate Libby Prison and goes to Virginia City to block a $5 million gold shipment that Southern sympathizers are preparing to smuggle through the Union lines to the hard-pressed Confederacy. Randolph Scott is the former commandant of Libby Prison who plans to send the gold to Richmond by wagon train.

In the unlikely role of a dance-hall entertainer functioning as a Southern spy, Miriam Hopkins

With Alan Hale and Guinn (Big Boy) Williams

has some stilted scenes with Flynn and ditto with Scott. Her less than buoyant singing and dancing of "Rally Round the Flag Boys" ("The Union Forever") could be attributed to the fact that in character as a Southern sympathizer, she was hard put to give her all in rendering a Northern song.

Even more ludicrous is the usually reliable Bogart, here cast as a half-breed outlaw with a not too convincing dialect.

Flynn eventually finds himself joining Scott and his group in defending the Richmond-bound gold wagon when Bogart's outlaws attack. After Scott is killed, Flynn has the gold buried to prevent its capture, hoping that it will be used to help rebuild the postwar South.

All the characters, with the exception of Jefferson Davis and President Lincoln (the latter in shadow only), are fictitious; but the basic incident of the gold shipment is true.

Following *Stagecoach*'s spacious use of Monument Valley backgrounds, *Virginia City*'s locations, as confirmed by assistant director Sherry Shourds, included the Painted Desert area in northern Arizona. A revamped Dodge City street at Calabasas Ranch also was put to good use.

One action highlight was a stunt (inspired by two stunts in *Stagecoach*) wherein Yakima Canutt (as in *Stagecoach*) leaps from one pair of horses pulling a coach to another pair, falls between the lead horses, hangs on to the coach tongue, drops to the ground with horses' hooves and coach wheels missing him on both sides, and finally, catching hold of the rear axle, pulls himself up.

Flynn overcame his material remarkably well, and Max Steiner contributed one of his most effective scores for a Flynn film.

Virginia City was nationally reissued in a package with *Dodge City* in 1951.

With Randolph Scott and Miriam Hopkins

The Sea Hawk

1940 A Warner Brothers-First National Picture. Directed by Michael Curtiz. Executive Producer: Hal B. Wallis. Associate Producer: Henry Blanke. Original Screenplay by Howard Koch and Seton I. Miller. Music by Erich Wolfgang Korngold. Director of Photography: Sol Polito. Dialogue Director: Jo Graham. Film Editor: George Amy. Art Director: Anton Grot. Sound: Francis J. Scheid. Costumes: Orry-Kelly. Make-up: Perc Westmore. Special Effects: Byron Haskin and H. F. Koenekamp. Orchestrations: Hugo Friedhofer, Milan Roder, Ray Heindorf, and Simon Bucharoff. Assistant Director: Jack Sullivan. Technical Advisers: Ali Hubert, Thomas Manners, and William Kiel. Fencing Master: Fred Cavens. Running time: 126 minutes.

With Gilbert Roland

CAST *Captain Geoffrey Thorpe*
ERROL FLYNN
Donna Maria Brenda MARSHALL
Don Jose Alvarez de Cordoba
Claude RAINS
Sir John Burleson Donald CRISP
Queen Elizabeth Flora ROBSON
Carl Pitt Alan HALE
Lord Wolfingham Henry DANIELL
Miss Latham Una O'Connor
Abbott James Stephenson
Captain Lopez Gilbert Roland
Danny Logan William Lundigan
Oliver Scott Julien Mitchell
King Philip II Montagu Love
Eli Matson J. M. Kerrigan
Martin Burke David Bruce
William Tuttle Clifford Brooke
Walter Boggs Clyde Cook
Inquisitor Fritz Leiber
Monty Preston Ellis Irving
Kroner Francis McDonald
Captain Mendoza Pedro de Cordoba
Peralta Ian Keith
Lieutenant Ortega Jack LaRue
Astronomer Halliwell Hobbes
Chartmaker Alec Craig
General Aguirre Victor Varconi
Captain Frobisher Robert Warwick
Slavemaster Harry Cording
Martin Barrett Frank Wilcox
Eph Winters Herbert Anderson
Arnold Cross Charles Irwin
Ben Rollins Edgar Buchanan
Captain Ortiz Frank Lackteen

THE SEA HAWK ranks as one of Flynn's best all-round films, and remains a beautiful picture to watch and to hear.

After *Captain Blood* proved to be a gold mine, Warners put writer Delmer Daves to work adapting another Rafael Sabatini novel, *The Sea Hawk,* a property acquired by Warners along with the entire First National Company in 1929-30. In 1924, First National had produced a costly, faith-

With Alan Hale

With Flora Robson

With Alec Craig

ful-to-the-book, and well-received version with Milton Sills.

Warners tabled the remake of *The Sea Hawk* for a while after Daves had finished the script. Seton I. Miller recalls that sometime later he sold an original story to the studio called *Beggars of the Sea,* dealing with the exploits of a character (suggested by Sir Francis Drake) who, along with other privateers, commanded marauding expedi-

With Alan Hale. Edgar Buchanan, Herbert Anderson, Julien Mitchell, Clifford Brooke, and Frank Wilcox

tions against the Spanish, taking rich booty from treasure ships and Spanish possessions in the Americas for the treasury of Queen Elizabeth. These "sea dogs," as they were called, actually were waging an undeclared war on Spanish shipping wherever they found it.

In 1939 Warners decided to produce *The Sea Hawk,* but dropped Sabatini's tale about a Cornish gentleman who became a Barbary corsair. Seton Miller's screenplay, *Beggars of the Sea,* was revised by Howard Koch, a playwright and radio writer—most notably of Orson Welles' famous "War of the Worlds" 1938 broadcast. Koch was handed *The Sea Hawk* as his first screen assignment and contributed some literate dialogue.

The term "sea dogs" was conveniently changed to "sea hawks," thereby refuting history and confusing Sabatini buffs, but giving a *raison d'être* to the saleable and dramatic title the studio decided to retain.

Even though they bestowed a then lavish budget of $1,700,000, the always cost-conscious Warner executives put into service many of *Elizabeth and Essex'* sets, set-dressing, and costumes.

An enormous new Warner sound stage was inaugurated for the film. It housed two newly built full-scale ships—one 165′ long, the other 135′—both surrounded by twelve feet of water. The big sea battle near the opening of the film between Captain Thorpe's (Flynn) ship, *Albatross,* and a Spanish galleon carrying the Spanish ambassador (Rains) and his niece (Marshall), remains an amazing and crammed-with-detail piece of film-making. The *Albatross* circles its prey, unleashing broadside after broadside. Then, after hitting the

With Fritz Leiber as the judge

With J. M. Kerrigan, James Stephenson, David Bruce, and Alan Hale.

With Brenda Marshall

galleon below the waterline, Thorpe and his men prepare to board the other ship by means of grappling hooks and lines from the rigging allowing them to swing from one deck to another. Then a furious melee involving cutlass, rapier, railing pin, and hand-to-hand combat takes place. Finally, the Spanish trumpeter is forced to blow surrender, just as the Sea Hawk is about to deliver the *coup de grâce* to the Spanish captain (Roland).

The full-scale ships were brilliantly intercut with models shot in a studio tank in a much more sophisticated and convincing fashion than in *Captain Blood*. Some sea-battle stock footage from the two *Captain Blood*s and the previous *Sea Hawk* was slipped in to augment the spectacle.

After being reprimanded in court by the queen for his actions on the ambassador's ship, Captain Thorpe sails to Panama to raid a treasure train in the jungle. For this expedition he carries Queen Elizabeth's private sanction and the love of the Spanish ambassador's niece. But the Spanish are warned by a spy in Elizabeth's court, and Thorpe

and his crew are captured and sentenced to serve as galley slaves on a Spanish galleon. They eventually escape and bring the queen written proof of the Spanish plan to send an armada against England. Before reaching the queen, Thorpe has a duel-to-the-death with spy-villain Lord Wolfingham (Daniell) that takes them through just about every room in the palace.

The Sea Hawk's rapier routine, by Fred Cavens, was more furiously paced and edited than *Robin Hood*'s. However, Flynn and Daniell were doubled extensively throughout the duel. Don Turner was Flynn's double on most of his swashbucklers, and Ned Davenport and Ralph Faulkner doubled for Daniell in *The Sea Hawk*. Candles, tables, candelabras, stairs, and shadows were used much as they had been in *Robin Hood*.

Erich Wolfgang Korngold's last score for an historical pageant was one of his best. The music splendidly captured the sweep and roll of sixteenth-century ships, the court pomp and intrigue of England and Spain, the dank jungles of Panama, and the oppressive Spanish galleys. It also included some beautiful love music, and one charming melody that Korngold later developed into an art-song.

As in the case of *Virginia City,* Technicolor and Olivia de Havilland were absent (both were included in earlier plans). But Sol Polito's high-contrast black-and-white photography is a high-water mark in opulent, dramatic lighting and composition in the classic style. His and Curtiz' love of the moving camera—in, out, down, up, sweeping, or cruising laterally—was extraordinarily effective.

Flora Robson reprised the role of Elizabeth that she had played in a 1936 British production, *Fire Over England,* a film which contained certain parallels in background and theme with *The Sea Hawk.* It is interesting to compare Bette Davis' and Robson's performances as Elizabeth. Both are intelligent and convincing, but Miss Robson conveys level-headedness with flashes of temper, while Davis projects distinctly neurotic and indecisive aspects of the character.

Flynn chose a relatively quiet, restrained delivery; he was gentlemanly, exercised cool judgment in leadership, and demonstrated embarrassed fumbling in the presence of ladies (other than the queen). It is a good, believable performance, and certainly he never looked as handsome and dashing before or after.

In 1947, after the box-office results of *The Spanish Main* and *Two Years Before the Mast,* *The Sea Hawk* was reissued nationally, with about ten minutes cut, on a dual bill with *The Sea Wolf,* a 1941 Warner version of the Jack London story. The program did big business everywhere, and precipitated the re-release of *Robin Hood* in the following year.

With Henry Daniell

With Flora Robson, Brenda Marshall, and Donald Crisp

With Flora Robson and Brenda Marshall

With Selmer Jackson and Moroni Olsen

Santa Fe Trail

1940 A Warner Brothers-First National Picture. Directed by Michael Curtiz. Executive Producer: Hal B. Wallis. Associate Producer: Robert Fellows. Original Screenplay by Robert Buckner. Music by Max Steiner. Director of Photography: Sol Polito. Dialogue Director: Jo Graham. Film Editor: George Amy. Art Director: John Hughes. Sound: Robert B. Lee. Costumes: Milo Anderson. Make-up: Perc Westmore. Special Effects: Byron Haskin and H. F. Koenekamp. Orchestrations: Hugo Friedhofer. Assistant Director: Jack Sullivan. Running time: 110 minutes.

With William Lundigan, Henry O'Neill, and Olivia de Havilland

97

With Ronald Reagan, Raymond Massey, Joe Sawyer, Ward Bond, and Gene Reynolds

With Olivia de Havilland and Ronald Reagan

CAST			
Jeb Stuart	ERROL FLYNN	*Barber Doyle*	Hobart Cavanaugh
Kit Carson Halliday		*Major Sumner*	Charles D. Brown
	OLIVIA de HAVILLAND	*Kitzmiller*	Joseph Sawyer
John Brown	Raymond MASSEY	*James Longstreet*	Frank Wilcox
George Armstrong Custer		*Townley*	Ward Bond
	Ronald REAGAN	*Shoubel Morgan*	Russell Simpson
Tex Bell	Alan HALE	*Gentry*	Charles Middleton
Bob Halliday	William Lundigan	*Jefferson Davis*	Erville Alderson
Rader	Van Heflin	*Conductor*	Spencer Charters
Jason Brown	Gene Reynolds	*Charlotte*	Suzanne Carnahan*
Cyrus Halliday	Henry O'Neill	*George Pickett*	William Marshall
Windy Brody	Guinn (Big Boy) Williams	*John Hood*	George Haywood
Oliver Brown	Alan Baxter	*Weiner*	Wilfred Lucas
Martin	John Litel	*J. Boyce Russell*	Russell Hicks
Robert E. Lee	Moroni Olsen		
Phil Sheridan	David Bruce	*later known as Susan Peters	

98

SANTA FE TRAIL, the third of several Westerns starring Flynn, and a total misnomer, dealt not with the important caravan route from Missouri to New Mexico, but with the Army versus John Brown, the radical abolitionist whose attempt to free the slaves cost a number of lives and helped indirectly to bring on the Civil War.

At the film's opening, Flynn, as the real-life cavalry commander James Ewell Brown (Jeb) Stuart, is seen graduating from West Point along with George Custer, Philip Sheridan, James Longstreet, George Pickett, and James Hood—all famous in Civil War history, but none of whom actually graduated the same year as Stuart (1854).

Many of the class go on to patrol the frontier from their post at Fort Leavenworth, Kansas. The conflict with Brown occupies much of the film, with the finale a re-creating of the events that took place at Harpers Ferry, West Virginia. Here Brown and his followers are beaten by Flynn and the militia after a bloody battle.

The film's oversimplified point of view seemed to be that Brown's passion to free the slaves was all right, but his violent measures were all wrong. Warners tried to please all sides with its theme, and played both ends against the middle.

The production was large scale, the action scenes contained the slam-bang Curtiz touch, the

With Ronald Reagan, Alan Hale, and Gene Reynolds

With Guinn (Big Boy) Williams, Alan Hale, and Ronald Reagan

With Raymond Massey, Van Heflin,
Joe Sawyer, and Ward Bond

love interest was arbitrary, and the cliché comic relief of Alan Hale and "Big Boy" Williams decidedly forced.

"Along the Santa Fe Trail," a good song written for the film, was used very sparingly in the background score and never sung.

Flynn's portrayal was the conventional dashing hero, with no attempt by him or the writer to characterize the real Jeb Stuart accurately.

With William Lundigan, David Bruce,
George Haywood, William Marshall,
Frank Wilcox, and Ronald Reagan

With Allen Jenkins

Footsteps in the Dark

1941   A Warner Brothers First National Picture. Directed by Lloyd Bacon. Executive Producer: Hal B. Wallis. Associate Producer: Robert Lord. Screenplay by Lester Cole and John Wexley. Based on the play *Blondie White* by Ladislaus Fodor; English adaptation by Bernard Merivale and Jeffrey Dell. Music by Frederick Hollander. Director of Photography: Ernest Haller. Dialogue Director: Hugh MacMullan. Film Editor: Owen Marks. Art Director: Max Parker. Sound: Francis J. Scheid. Gowns: Howard Shoup. Make-up: Perc Westmore. Special Effects: Rex Wimpy. Dance Director: Robert Vreeland. Assistant Director: Frank Heath. Running time: 96 minutes.

With Brenda Marshall and
Lucile Watson

With William Frawley, Ralph Bellamy, and Allen Jenkins

bucklers or epic Westerns—Warners finally acceded to Flynn's constant demands to do a light, modern comedy.

Footsteps in the Dark was the comedy, but a poor one. Once again Flynn seemed jinxed in his nonheroic vehicles.

The plot has to do with a well-to-do investment counselor (Flynn) who secretly plays amateur criminologist in order to write satirical detective novels. His search for story material takes him on nightly prowls which he conceals from his wife (Marshall). Along the way he encounters a jewelry smuggler who is found dead from acute alcoholism the following day. Flynn, in trying to track down the murderer, has an encounter with a burlesque stripper (Patrick), at which point he has some painful scenes posing as a wealthy Texas cattleman. Finally it becomes apparent that Ralph Bellamy, as a dentist for whom oral surgery is merely a cover-up, did it.

Obviously patterned somewhat in *The Thin Man* mode, much of the material was ridiculous and old-fashioned, with Flynn appearing more foolish than funny.

CAST		
Francis Warren	ERROL FLYNN
Rita Warren	Brenda MARSHALL
Dr. Davis	Ralph BELLAMY
Inspector Mason	Alan HALE
Blondie White	Lee Patrick
Wilfred	Allen Jenkins
Mrs. Archer	Lucile Watson
Hopkins	William Frawley
Monahan	Roscoe Karns
Carruthers	Grant Mitchell
June Brewster	Maris Wrixon
Fissue	Noel Madison
Ace Vernon	Jack LaRue
Ahmed	Turhan Bey
Gus	Frank Faylen
Jackson	Garry Owen
Mrs. Belgarde	Sarah Edwards
Harrow	Frank Wilcox
Horace	Olaf Hytten
Willis	Harry Hayden
Coroner	John Dilson
Harlan	Creighton Hale

A FTER doing seven period pictures in a row in less than three years—most of them swash-

With Frank Faylen, Allen Jenkins, William Frawley, Lucile Watson, and Brenda Marshall

Dive Bomber

1941 A Warner Brothers-First National Picture. Technicolor. Directed by Michael Curtiz. Executive Producer: Hal B. Wallis. Associate Producer: Robert Lord. Screenplay by Frank Wead and Robert Buckner. Based on an original story by Frank Wead. Music by Max Steiner. Directors of Photography: Bert Glennon and Winton C. Hoch. Aerial Photography: Elmer Dyer and Charles Marshall. Dialogue Director: Hugh MacMullan. Film Editor: George Amy. Art Director: Robert Haas. Sound: Francis J. Scheid. Make-up: Perc Westmore. Special Effects: Byron Haskin and Rex Wimpy. Orchestrations: Hugo Friedhofer. Assistant Director: Sherry Shourds. Chief Pilot: Paul Mantz. Aeronautical Technical Adviser: S. H. Warner, Commander, USN. Medical Technical Adviser: J. R. Poppen, Captain (MC), USN. Technicolor Color Director: Natalie Kalmus. Unit Manager: Al Alleborn. Running time: 133 minutes.

With Ralph Bellamy

CAST *Lieutenant Douglas Lee* ERROL FLYNN
Commander Joe Blake
                        FRED MacMURRAY
Dr. Lance Rogers   Ralph BELLAMY
Linda Fisher   Alexis SMITH
Art Lyons   Robert Armstrong
Tim Griffin   Regis Toomey
Lucky James   Allen Jenkins
John Thomas Anthony   Craig Stevens
Chubby   Herbert Anderson
Senior Flight Surgeon Moroni Olsen
Mrs. James   Dennie Moore
Swede Larson   Louis Jean Heydt
Corps Man   Cliff Nazarro
Helen   Ann Doran
Senior Flight Surgeon Addison Richards
Admiral   Russell Hicks
Admiral   Howard Hickman
Pilots: William Hopper, Charles Drake, Gig Young, Larry Williams, Garland Smith, Tom Skinner, Tom Seidel, Gaylord Pendleton, Lyle Moraine, Garrett Craig, James Anderson, Stanley Smith, David Newell, Alan Hale, Jr., Sol Gorss, Don Turner

BETWEEN the release of *The Dawn Patrol* in December of 1938 and *Dive Bomber* in August 1941, a major change in war attitude and air

With Fred MacMurray, Ralph Bellamy, and Robert Armstrong

104

progress in the United States had taken place. Pacifism was out, and the big build-up to America's entry into World War II, which had commenced in 1939, was in full swing. *Dive Bomber,* one of many films of the time glorifying the service branches, was given Technicolor, big-budget treatment, and full cooperation of the Naval Air Corps.

The picture constantly waivered. There was an interesting, rather detailed examination of the then new techniques in estimating a flyer's fitness, in solving the problems of "blacking out" when a pilot pulls out of a power dive, and in overcoming the hazards of stratospheric flying. Truly breathtaking formation flying, enhanced further by smogless Technicolor, was used in abundance. This dramatic and topical material was contrasted with flat story development in combination with artless "romantic interest."

MacMurray played a flyer who helps Flight Surgeon Flynn design a high-altitude pressure suit, which eventually costs MacMurray his life, but opens up new vistas in flying.

A good deal of the film was photographed at the Naval Air Station in San Diego and in the air amid billowing California clouds. Additional material was filmed at Pensacola Naval Air Station and aboard the aircraft carrier *Enterprise.*

With Ralph Bellamy

With Fred MacMurray and Alexis Smith

They Died with Their Boots On

With Joe Sawyer and Arthur Kennedy

1942 A Warner Brothers-First National Picture. Directed by Raoul Walsh. Executive Producer: Hal B. Wallis. Associate Producer: Robert Fellows. Original Screenplay by Wally Kline and Aeneas MacKenzie. Music by Max Steiner. Director of Photography: Bert Glennon. Dialogue Director: Edward A. Blatt. Film Editor: William Holmes. Art Director: John Hughes. Sound: Dolph Thomas. Gowns: Milo Anderson. Make-up: Perc Westmore. Assistant Director: Russell Saunders. Technical Adviser: Lieutenant Colonel J. G. Taylor, US Army, Retired. Running time: 140 minutes.

CAST

George Armstrong Custer	
	ERROL FLYNN
Elizabeth Bacon Custer	
	OLIVIA de HAVILLAND
Ned Sharp	Arthur KENNEDY
California Joe	Charley GRAPEWIN
Samuel Bacon	Gene LOCKHART
Crazy Horse	Anthony Quinn
Major Romulus Taipe	Stanley Ridges
General Philip Sheridan	John Litel
William Sharp	Walter Hampden
General Winfield Scott	
	Sydney Greenstreet
Fitzhugh Lee	Regis Toomey
Callie	Hattie McDaniel
Lieutenant Butler	G. P. Huntley, Jr.
Captain Webb	Frank Wilcox
Sergeant Doolittle	Joseph Sawyer
Senator Smith	Minor Watson
President Grant	Joseph Crehan
Salesman	Irving Bacon
Captain McCook	Selmer Jackson
Corporal Smith	Eddie Acuff
Captain Riley	George Eldredge
Station Master	Spencer Charters
Clergyman	Hobart Bosworth
Colonel of 1st Michigan	Russell Hicks
Major Smith	Hugh Sothern
Lieutenant Davis	John Ridgely
Lieutenant Roberts	Gig Young
Mrs. Sharp	Aileen Pringle
Mrs. Taipe	Anna Q. Nilsson
Grant's Secretary	Frank Ferguson

FOLLOWING *Dive Bomber*, Flynn was scheduled to appear in *The Constant Nymph* with Joan Leslie, but this was deferred for *They Died with Their Boots On*. *Nymph* was made a short

With Stanley Ridges and Sydney Greenstreet

while later with Charles Boyer in the role originally assigned to Flynn.

Having invented an entirely new background to lead up to *The Charge of the Light Brigade,* Warner Brothers apparently assumed there was little harm in heavily distorting history for the story behind General George Armstrong Custer and his famous last stand, a story, incidentally, which had never been dealt with previously in a major film.

Custer was a complex and controversial man, and his participation in the events that culminated in the battle at Little Big Horn has brought forth a multitude of interpretations. The Warner film presented a version made largely out of whole cloth, and filled with romantic trappings in order to have it fit the hero mold of Errol Flynn.

In bare outline, the script is reasonably true to the milestones in Custer's life. In motivation, character, and detail it is rather at odds with history. Custer is first seen entering West Point, where considerable footage shows his trials and tribulations at that institution. By fictional means he then becomes one of the most brilliant cavalry leaders of the Civil War, a hero who leads three successive charges that virtually annihilate his own Michigan Brigade. After the war and a period of forced retirement, he is placed in charge of the Seventh Cavalry, guardian of the Dakota Territory in the 1870s. Here he is shown as being sympathetic to the Indians. The heavies are fabricated scheming whites who spread a false rumor

of a gold strike in a territory ceded to the Indians—the Black Hills. Having promised the Indians to keep the white man out of the Black Hills, Custer (via Warner motivation) is forced to go into the area to stop the retaliation of the tribes. On June 25, 1876, he and approximately 225 of his command were killed by the Sioux and Cheyenne near the Little Big Horn River. The last sentence is fact.

With Olivia de Havilland

Many of Custer's personal traits were well within Flynn's grasp. Custer has been described as tall, lithe, and slender, a man of rare charm, mischievously given to pranks, gregarious and boyish. He spent much of his leisure time writing. Few of Custer's complexities were delineated in the script; he was presented as a relatively standard devil-may-care adventure hero, who later becomes restless when prematurely inactive in his profession. Still later in the West, he is shown as a stern disciplinarian, a man of honor, and something of an idealist.

Flynn did well, considering the conditions and circumstances. His scenes with Olivia de Havilland (as Custer's wife) were a cut above similar ones in *Santa Fe Trail,* but not as effective as their *Robin Hood* interludes. This was their last of eight films in six years. As a screen team of the late thirties, they appeared together as regularly as William Powell and Myrna Loy, Jeanette MacDonald and Nelson Eddy, Johnny Weissmuller and Maureen O'Sullivan.

The scene in which Custer says good-by to his wife as he prepares to go off to his death is rather touching. Flynn knew that his co-star had been anxious to play more important roles than "the girl" in his action dramas, and he knew that *Boots* would probably be their last film together. He

also had been infatuated with Olivia for quite some time; so watching them in their well-played final scene has a multiple significance.

With Arthur Kennedy

With Olivia de Havilland

In other respects, *Boots* generally manages, through its variety of incidents, time, and locale, to hold interest. The picture was produced on a big scale, but Custer's Last Stand, filmed at Agoura (Lasky Mesa), does not measure up to the incredible cinematics of *The Charge of the Light Brigade*. It employs masses effectively, but the mosaic of images that was so exceptional in *The Charge* is not as powerful here.

Featured throughout *Boots* was the true regimental battle song of the Seventh Cavalry, "Garry Owen." An Irish quick-marching and drinking

With Anthony Quinn

song, it was adopted by the regiment about 1867 and remained Custer's favorite.

Michael Curtiz was slated to direct *They Died with Their Boots On,* but he and Flynn were not getting along, and after *Dive Bomber* they decided not to work together in the future. Curtiz—known as "the work-horse of Warners"—was a hard-driving craftsman who reveled in a back-breaking schedule day after day, and expected everyone else on his films to display the same strength, vitality, and singleness of purpose. He reputedly was ruthless in his staging of action scenes—demanding thrills, and apparently not too concerned about possible dangers to player and/or

animal. By the time Flynn had finished his twelfth film with the director, he insisted on a less strenuous schedule and more relaxed working conditions than were possible with Curtiz. Also, apparently Curtiz baited Flynn on occasion.

Raoul Walsh, another rough-hewn action specialist (his credits include the original silent versions of *The Thief of Bagdad* and *What Price Glory?;* and *The Roaring Twenties* and *Captain Horatio Hornblower,* among others) was probably the only director at Warners who could follow Curtiz' act on Flynn vehicles. He was certainly tough, but not as overly demanding of cast and crew.

In September, 1941, while *Boots* was still in production, Flynn collapsed in the elevator of a medical building from what physicians told the press was "nervous exhaustion."

With Arthur Kennedy, Patrick O'Moore, and Alan Hale

Desperate Journey

1942 A Warner Brothers First National Picture. Directed by Raoul Walsh. Executive Producer: Hal B. Wallis. Associate Producer: Jack Saper. Original Screenplay by Arthur T. Horman. Music by Max Steiner. Director of Photography: Bert Glennon. Dialogue Director: Hugh MacMullan. Film Editor: Rudi Fehr. Art Director: Carl Jules Weyl. Sound: C. A. Riggs. Gowns: Milo Anderson. Make-up: Perc Westmore. Special Effects: Edwin DuPar. Orchestrations: Hugo Friedhofer. Assistant Director: Russell Saunders. Technical Adviser on RAF Sequences: S/L O. Cathcart-Jones, RCAF. Running time: 107 minutes.

With Arthur Kennedy, Alan Hale,
Ronald Reagan, and Ronald Sinclair

CAST *Flight Lieutenant Terence Forbes*
              ERROL FLYNN
        Flying Officer Johnny Hammond
              RONALD REAGAN
        Kaethe Brahms   Nancy COLEMAN
        Major Otto Baumeister
              Raymond MASSEY
        Flight Sergeant Kirk Edwards
              Alan HALE
        Flying Officer Jed Forrest
              Arthur KENNEDY
        Flight Sergeant Lloyd Hollis
              Ronald Sinclair
        Dr. Mather   Albert Basserman
        Preuss   Sig Rumann

Squadron Leader Lane Ferris
                          Patrick O'Moore
Dr. Herman Brahms   Felix Basch
Frau Brahms   Ilka Gruning
Frau Raeder   Elsa Basserman
Captain Coswick   Charles Irwin
Squadron Leader Clark   Richard Fraser
Kruse   Robert O. Davis
Heinrich Schwartzmuller Henry Victor
Assistant Plotting Officer Bruce Lester
Wing Commander   Lester Matthews
Hesse   Kurt Katch
Gestapo   Hans Schumm
German Co-Pilot   Helmut Dantine
Squadron Commander   Barry Bernard

With Alan Hale, Arthur Kennedy,
Ronald Reagan, Ronald Sinclair,
and Raymond Massey

With Nancy Coleman

NOT to be taken seriously, *Desperate Journey* tells in Rover Boy-like fashion the exploits of an RAF bomber crew who, having destroyed an objective, is brought down by antiaircraft fire in Germany. Five members survive and attempt to make their way through Germany back to England. En route they destroy a chemical plant, engage in open car chases, narrow escapes, assorted violence, and general derring-do.

The crew is continuously pursued by a Nazi colonel (Massey), who realizes each member knows the whereabouts and *modus operandi* of an underground Messerschmitt factory, commanded by the colonel. The Nazis attempting to track down the intrepid adventurers seemed to be composed of the halt, the blind, and the mentally deficient.

After the five have been reduced to three, they steal a bomber as it is about to take off to demolish London's water works.

Even before he lands the plane on home soil, Flynn, the flight lieutenant, after two hours of enough adventure to last any ten men a lifetime, announces eagerly: "Now for Australia and a crack at the Japs!"

The five RAF boys are an Australian (Flynn), an American (Reagan), a Canadian (Kennedy), a Scottish veteran of World War I (Hale), and a young Englishman (Sinclair).

Director Walsh's customary adroitness in handling fast-paced melodrama is in plentiful evidence, but the superabundance and ludicrousness of the heroics—to say nothing of the extraordinary luck of the lads—takes its toll in one's ability to accept the narrative. However, much of it is good, noisy fun if a willing suspension of disbelief is called upon.

Desperate Journey was playing theaters when the Flynn rape scandal made the headlines. The box office did not suffer; on the contrary, it was aided considerably. One line in the film's previews of coming attractions brought down the house and was quickly deleted: "They know but one command—attack!"

114

Gentleman Jim

1942 A Warner Brothers First National Picture. Directed by Raoul Walsh. Produced by Robert Buckner. Screenplay by Vincent Lawrence and Horace McCoy. Based on the life of James J. Corbett, and on Corbett's autobiography, *The Roar of the Crowd*. Music by Heinz Roemheld. Director of Photography: Sid Hickox. Dialogue Director: Hugh Cummings. Film Editor: Jack Killifer. Art Director: Ted Smith. Sound: C. A. Riggs. Gowns: Milo Anderson. Make-up: Perc Westmore. Montages: Don Siegel and James Leicester. Orchestrations: Ray Heindorf. Assistant Director: Russell Saunders. Technical Adviser: Ed Cochrane. Unit Manager: Frank Mattison. Running time: 104 minutes.

CAST

James J. Corbett	ERROL FLYNN
Victoria Ware	ALEXIS SMITH
Walter Lowrie	Jack CARSON
Pat Corbett	Alan HALE
Clinton DeWitt	John Loder
Billy Delaney	William Frawley
Buck Ware	Minor Watson
John L. Sullivan	Ward Bond
Anna Held	Madeleine LeBeau
Harry Watson	Rhys Williams
Father Burke	Arthur Shields
Ma Corbett	Dorothy Vaughan
George Corbett	James Flavin
Harry Corbett	Pat Flaherty
Judge Geary	Wallis Clark
Mary Corbett	Marilyn Phillips
Jack Burke	Art Foster
President McInnes	Edwin Stanley
Colis Huntington	Henry O'Hara
Charles Crocker	Harry Crocker
Governor Stanford	Frank Mayo
Smith	Carl Harbaugh
Sutro	Fred Kelsey
Joe Choynski	Sammy Stein
Gurney	Charles Wilson
Renaud	Jean Del Val
Donovan	William B. Davidson
Jake Kilrain	Mike Mazurki

DURING his film career Flynn portrayed seven real-life characters: Fletcher Christian, Essex, Jeb Stuart, Custer, Edward, the Black Prince,

John Barrymore, and James J. Corbett, the first scientific boxer and the first heavyweight champion of the world under the present Marquis of Queensberry rules.

Flynn was a perfect choice to play Corbett: the boxer was of Irish parentage, twice expelled from school for boyish pranks, married to an actress at nineteen and later divorced, 6'1", a slim 178 pounds during his heyday, and quick-thinking. He introduced "dancing" footwork in the ring as well as an elusive, side-stepping defensive tactic, and he later appeared on the stage and in films.

Corbett, born and raised in south San Francisco, is portrayed in the film as a young bank clerk who witnesses an illegal prize fight in 1887. The event results in projecting him into the Olympic Club, and then, through a series of circumstances, he becomes a professional fighter.

The boxing scenes in *Gentleman Jim* were well done and excitingly staged. The factual fight between Corbett and Joe Choynski on a barge in San Francisco Bay (re-created on *The Sea Hawk's* ship stage, complete with water and a vessel from the 1941 *Sea Wolf* in the background), and the climactic twenty-one round encounter for the championship with John L. Sullivan (Bond) in New Orleans were re-created with spirit and considerable detail.

With Rhys Williams, Alexis Smith, and Wallis Clark

With Jack Carson, William Frawley, Alan Hale, and Arthur Shields

116

Flynn obviously approached the assignment seriously. He was rarely, if ever, doubled in the ring footage. Ed Cochrane, sports writer and Corbett authority, and Mushy Callahan, one-time junior welterweight champ, worked closely with Flynn in an attempt to parallel Corbett's style. The boxer's stance, footwork, left jabs (he was right-handed), left hook (which he introduced), feinting, slipping, side-stepping, et al, were all in evidence.

In other respects, as the bright, brash, confident fellow with the "gentleman's demeanor," Flynn sustained and made believable his characterization. But, unfortunately, the vehicle was annoy-ingly uneven. Due to lack of clearances and presumably other reasons, the writers invented a wholly fictitious and unbelievable love interest. Also, they introduced other incidents and situations that wandered far from authenticity. Prolonged footage of Jim's caricatured Irish family, accompanied by painful attempts at humor tend to mar the film.

Despite the negative facets, *Gentleman Jim* must be included in any Flynn retrospective, and was one of the actor's personal favorites, as he states in his autobiography.

Flynn collapsed on the set during filming of the John L. Sullivan bout. The press release stated

With Alan Hale

117

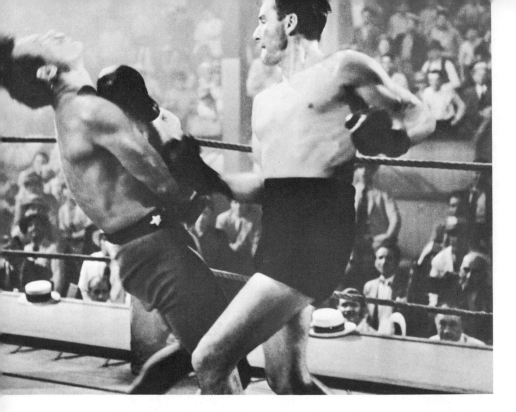

With Ward Bond

that he was suffering .from "fatigue." Several weeks earlier he had been turned down for duty in the Navy and Army due to what doctors termed "athlete's heart."

The first impact of the 1942 rape scandal helped the box office on *Desperate Journey,* so Warners rushed *Gentleman Jim* into theaters, not wanting to risk waiting for the outcome of the trial, which was scheduled to commence three months later. *Gentleman Jim* did well, but the studio waited with trepidation for the trial and its effect on the almost completed *Edge of Darkness.* They had recently signed Flynn to a new seven-year contract, and had approximately $3 million invested in *Desperate Journey, Gentleman Jim,* and *Edge of Darkness.*

With Ward Bond

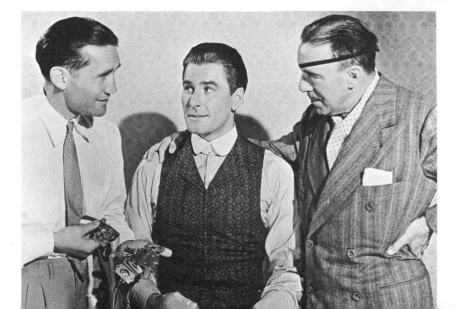

Flynn with his trainer, Mushy Callahan, and director Raoul Walsh

Part Three

The Slow Deflation

As a man in his mid-thirties, Flynn was on almost everyone's list of Hollywood's most handsome actors

FROM the rape trial to his death sixteen years later, Errol Flynn was continuously ridiculed about two things: his amorous exploits and his screen heroics. The humor leveled against him on both counts became absurd. In public he was bothered by women trying to flirt and men who were curious to find out if he was really tough. In most of these situations he could charm his way out, and occasionally he would resort to using his fists when men made it impossible for him to back away. Flynn knew how to fight, and from his days as a roustabout in the South Seas he also knew tricks to quickly incapacitate an opponent. His favorite ruse in order to avoid having to use his skill as a boxer was to bring his heel down sharply on the arch of the other man's foot. Trouble seemed to follow Flynn, and he became resigned to it, admitting that while he was greatly afraid of danger, he felt drawn to it as a moth to flame.

Radio comedians, newspaper columnists, and scandal magazines became the bane of Flynn. But he did little to counteract whatever ludicrous impressions were spread about himself; he seemed to laugh along with the fun-pokers and he gave them grist for their mills. Some of the best cracks came from Flynn himself, such as, "I'm thinking of giving up acting and devoting myself to full-time litigation." Only once did he have his lawyers prepare a case against a magazine: in 1957 *Confidential* printed a particularly scurrilous account of his sex life. Flynn won the case, but received only a fraction of the money he sued for. At the time he made a statement that surprised many people, "It's not me I'm worried about, it's my kids. Nobody likes their kids to go to school and have a copy of *Confidential* pushed in their faces and listen to jeers, 'Ha, here's your old man.' They suffer, these little ones."

It was Flynn's custom to mask his truths with jests; this he would do rather than allow people to suspect his true sentiments. He once said, "Women won't let me stay single and I won't let myself stay married," thereby neatly summing up his whole attitude toward marriage. His second wife was Nora Eddington, whom he spotted at the Los Angeles Hall of Justice during the rape trial. Nora was working at the cigar counter, and once he was acquitted he had one of his friends arrange a meeting. Nora was then eighteen and the daughter of Jack Eddington, the secretary to the sheriff. A pretty redhead with green-blue eyes, Nora was Mrs. Flynn within the year, although Flynn seemed reluctant to admit to the marriage. At first

Flynn with his wife Nora Eddington in March, 1945

he set up a separate residence for Nora, possibly trying to institute a new concept of marriage—how to be single though married. In time Nora moved into the Flynn mansion off Mulholland Drive, high in the Hollywood hills, and during a marriage that lasted six years, she bore him two daughters, Deirdre and Rory.

Nora divorced Flynn in 1949, and shortly thereafter married crooner Dick Haymes. Flynn had proved himself not only a difficult man to live with, but because of an increasing addiction to narcotics, a dangerous man. Some time after the divorce, when the ill feelings had abated, Flynn would occasionally visit and keep up a correspondence with Nora. The question she is often asked about Flynn concerns his bravery: was he as courageous in real life as he often appeared on screen? "I found he was brave in almost everything he did, possibly because he would try everything there was to try or do. He wasn't afraid of anything, particularly if there was a challenge to it—he would do anything."

The willingness to try anything led Flynn to narcotics. "He felt he could master everything," says Nora, "and he felt he could stop any time he wanted to. He told me he had no intention of being an addict. He enjoyed the sensations it gave him and he described them to me. I don't think he ever believed he couldn't stop. But he went on

and on, and it does catch up with you. He kept it up until he died; in fact I think that's what killed him." In Nora's view it was impossible to contain Flynn. "He was out to live and live he did. The only time he wasn't living was when he was asleep, and even then I think he dreamt well."

For Errol Flynn the one great escape was the ocean, his love of the sea was his hold on sanity—it was in the water and on the water that he felt at home and at ease. One of the first things he did when he began to make money as an actor was to buy a ketch. He named her *Sirocco* after the old yacht he had owned in Australia. There is an unwritten law among mariners never to name one ship after another, and Flynn probably regretted having ignored that law. The *Sirocco* figured prominently in the rape trial, one of the girls having charged Flynn with assaulting her below decks. Pictures and blueprints of the boat were presented in court as evidence, and one of the many jokes that sprang from the trial came from the girl's claim to have gazed at the moon from a *Sirocco* porthole during the struggle with her virtue. Flynn sold the boat soon after the trial and bought another a couple of years later.

The boat Flynn next acquired was a handsome schooner that had been used by the Navy during the Second World War. He called her *Zaca*, and for him it was not a name idly bestowed—*Zaca* is

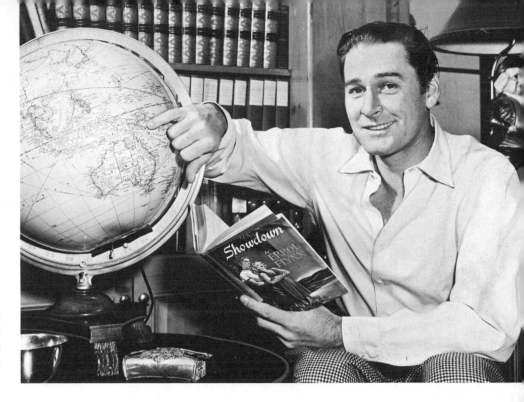

Flynn in February, 1946, when his book Showdown *appeared. Here he points to the locale of the story, the New Guinea waters — an area he knew well.*

the Samoan word for peace. Almost 120′ in length, and mounting two masts, she could sail or be driven by her motors. The *Zaca* was a sailor's dream come true and Flynn loved her. It was his plan to eventually sail her to the South Seas, but she never made that trip. Most of the time her home port was Port Antonio, Jamaica, and later Majorca.

Another thing that interested Flynn greatly was writing. He had started writing newspaper articles in New Guinea, and when he became well known as an actor he wrote for a number of magazines. His first book, *Beam Ends,* was possibly his best work, an amusing account of his voyage up the east coast of Australia in 1930. He co-authored a screenplay called *The White Rajah* and sold it to Warners, but they never used it. Flynn took credit for the screenplay of *Adventures of Captain Fabian,* a limp and unoriginal story. His most ambitious work, aside from his autobiography with which he was helped, was a novel called *Showdown,* published in 1946.

Showdown was faintly autobiographical. Concerning the adventures of a young Irishman in the South Seas, Flynn drew upon his considerable knowledge of the area. Whatever success the book had was due to the name of its author. The critics were rough on it, saying it was overwritten and tedious. A *New York Herald Tribune* reporter asked Flynn why he had spent so much time writing a book when he obviously didn't need the

money or further fame. Replied Flynn, "I got more of a kick out of writing it than I do out of making pictures. That's the only explanation I can give. It helped me get rid of a sense of futility."

The Second World War brought great changes in public taste, and many film stars who had hitherto been powerful names at the box office found themselves with not quite the same power, Errol Flynn among them. He continued to star in major features, but they no longer drew the enthusiasm of as many fans as in previous times. In 1947, in an attempt to recapture former glory, Warners decided to gamble a large budget on *Adventures of Don Juan* and give the public the Flynn they had so admired in vehicles like *Robin Hood* and *The Sea Hawk.* It was a twilight decision; Flynn by now was thirty-eight but much older in body.

The man assigned to direct *Don Juan* was Vincent Sherman. Because of Flynn's tardiness and his irresponsibility, the relationship between the actor and the studio had become strained and Sherman had been warned by other directors of what to expect. By the end of the picture Sherman would know what they meant—Flynn's lateness, his absences, and his drinking had inflated the budget of *Don Juan* by half a million dollars.

Vincent Sherman came to view Flynn as a sensitive and highly complicated man who wanted to be recognized as a good actor but at the same time made fun of the whole business of acting. "I think Errol was a good actor, and there are

Flynn as Don Juan

not many who can do what he did. Not every actor can be a swashbuckler. He knew how to wear a costume with grace, he knew how to move, he had a charming manner and an enchanting quality when he met a woman, both on and off screen. He had a graciousness about him. I respected the talent he had because you don't find that talent easily. The unfortunate thing is he denigrated himself. If you said, 'Errol, there's nobody who can wear a costume like you, or handle a sword like you, or come into a queen's court and make a bow like you,' well, for him that was almost insulting. He didn't accept that as part of a talent. He didn't really appreciate himself."

Observing Flynn in the role of Don Juan, Vincent Sherman was able to assess the man playing a part with which he was so closely identified. "Flynn had a complicated regard for women, and possibly it stemmed from his relationship with his parents. He spoke with great respect for his father, but he expressed less than a son's love for his mother. It's easy for the gossips to dismiss him as a Don Juan, as a philanderer, but I think he basically feared women and distrusted them. He once told me he enjoyed a closeness and a companionship with men that he could never achieve with women."

By 1950 Flynn's career was slipping badly, but he was not alone in his dilemma. Television had become entrenched and Hollywood was in a panic. Few stars were attracting people to the theaters and the studio executives decided to cut

Flynn with three of his four children—his two daughters by Nora Eddington, Rory and Deirdre, and his son by Lili Damita, Sean.

their payrolls and give the axe to their most expensive talents.

Errol Flynn's residency in Hollywood ended in mid-1952, and for the remaining seven years of his life he would be a man of no fixed abode, largely a yacht dweller. His decision to leave Hollywood was brought on by more reasons than the decline in the industry. By now his financial affairs were beginning to be severe; he was constantly behind with his alimony payments and gradually getting into debt with back taxes to the government. Flynn moved to Europe for two reasons: one being his greater popularity there than in America, and secondly his plan to set up his own company.

At this stage in his life Errol Flynn was a man in transition, and it was far more than a matter of geography. There was a gradual coarsening in his face and a deadening of expression in the eyes due to alcohol and drugs. He was unable to perform as athletically as before. Perhaps the biggest change was mental. He continued to put up a brave front, but there were signs of despondency and bitterness. In a magazine article published at this time, Flynn made some revealing comments about himself:

When I first came to Hollywood, I enjoyed whatever fame I had, but gradually it began to pall on me. The days of my poverty and vagabondage come back to me now with a nostalgia that has the force of a blow. It's pleasant to remember I had few worries then and practically no financial responsibility. I felt rich when I had accumulated twenty-five dollars. No one had invested millions in me, and the jobs of hundreds of others were not dependent on me. It was pleasant to be carefree and irresponsible—but these days there doesn't seem to be any geography left in which to be carefree and irresponsible. Naturally restless, however, I frequently find myself rebelling inwardly at the deadly routine of picture-making. I get the feeling that life is slipping by me—the time is passing and I am not living fully.

Edge of Darkness

1943   A Warner Brothers-First National Picture. Directed by Lewis Milestone. Produced by Henry Blanke. Screenplay by Robert Rossen. Based on the novel by William Woods. Music by Franz Waxman. Director of Photography: Sid Hickox. Dialogue Director: Herschel Daugherty. Film Editor: David Weisbart. Art Director: Robert Haas. Set Decorator: Julia Heron. Sound: Everett A. Brown. Gowns: Orry-Kelly. Make-up: Perc Westmore. Special Effects: Lawrence Butler and Willard Van Enger. Montages: Don Siegel and James Leicester. Orchestrations: Leonid Raab. Assistant Directors: Sherry Shourds and James McMahon. Technical Advisers: Frank U. Peter Pohlenz, E. Wessel Klausen, and Gerard Lambert. Unit Manager: Lou Baum. Running time: 120 minutes.

CAST

Gunnar Brogge	ERROL FLYNN
Karen Stensgard	ANN SHERIDAN
Dr. Martin Stensgard	Walter HUSTON
Katja	Nancy COLEMAN
Captain Koenig	Helmut DANTINE
Gerd Bjarnesen	Judith ANDERSON
Anna Stensgard	Ruth GORDON
Johann Stensgard	John Beal
Sixtus Andresen	Morris Carnovsky
Kaspar Torgersen	Charles Dingle
Lars Malken	Roman Bohnen
Pastor Aalesen	Richard Fraser
Knut Osterholm	Art Smith
Hammer	Tom Fadden
Major Ruck	Henry Brandon
Paul	Tonio Selwart
Frida	Helene Thimig
Jensen	Frank Wilcox
Mortensen	Francis Pierlot
Mrs. Mortensen	Lottie Williams
Petersen	Monte Blue
Solveig Brategaard	Dorothy Tree
Hulda	Virginia Christine
Helmut	Henry Rowland
German Captain	Kurt Katch
German Aviator	Kurt Kreuger
German Soldier	Peter Van Eyck

E DGE OF DARKNESS begins with a series of scenes reminiscent of the intriguing opening of *Beau Geste:* The crew of a German patrol boat during World War II makes the discovery that the

With Ann Sheridan

entire Nazi occupational force of a Norwegian town and apparently every resident have been killed in a battle of extermination. Dead Norwegians are piled high and surrounded by dead Nazis, and a Norwegian flag flies valiantly over the German garrison. Then, in a flashback which occupies the remainder of the film, the events leading up to the rebellion are unfolded.

Flynn is a Norwegian fisherman who is the ringleader of the underground movement, and Sheridan is his fiancée, who, late in the film, is raped by a German soldier.

With Walter Huston and
Ann Sheridan

The film's emphasis is not on Flynn and Sheridan, but rather on the ensemble of leading townspeople and the frustrated Nazi commandant (Dantine). There is a highly respected physician (Huston) who is one of the last of the community's citizens to join the underground, his shy, retiring wife (Gordon), their weak, traitorous son (Beal), the opportunistic businessman who sells out to the Germans (Dingle), the innkeeper (Anderson), a kind of Norwegian Madame Defarge whose hatred of the enemy is intensified by their killing her husband, and a fearless, philosophical schoolmaster (Carnovsky), whose ivory tower is destroyed.

The primary tactic of the underground is passive resistance until the time comes when, aided by British bullets, the organized rebellion breaks out into a dramatic show of strength. The latter scenes, in which the German garrison is attacked and wiped out by the Norwegians, were handled with Milestone's always effective staging, timing, filmic strength, and eye for detail in this kind of material.

Edge of Darkness was based on a 1942 novel of the same name, but was considerably changed in both characters and tone when adapted for the screen. The book's author, like John Steinbeck for his somewhat similar *The Moon is Down,* was accused of an unfortunately sympathetic consideration of the Nazi character, whereas, in retrospect, it appears that he was trying to be as objective as possible. In so doing, he condemned the

With Ann Sheridan

*With Art Smith, Roman Bohnen,
and Ann Sheridan*

forces that motivate the action of his Nazi characters, without condemning the characters themselves. The film recast the enemy more along the traditional villain line.

There were three other films released within a few months that dealt with occupied Norway: *The Avengers, Commandos Strike at Dawn,* and *The Moon is Down. Edge of Darkness*, coming late in the cycle, received good to excellent reviews at the time, and coincided with the rising tide of rebellious outbreaks in occupied countries.

Some of the exteriors were photographed in the Northern California town of Monterey and the surrounding area. The company was idle for weeks waiting for the thick coastal fog to clear. Finally, the remainder of the film was photographed at the studio in Burbank.

Edge of Darkness is not, strictly speaking, a Flynn vehicle. He was still working on the film when the rape scandal broke, but managed to turn in a subdued, believable performance. He always got along well with Sheridan, and their scenes together had more spark than scenes he shared with some of his other leading ladies.

*With Walter Huston, Ann Sheridan,
Judith Anderson, Francis Pierlot,
and Art Smith*

129

The bartender is Monte Blue

Thank Your Lucky Stars

1943   A Warner Brothers-First National Picture. Directed by David Butler. Produced by Mark Hellinger. Screenplay by Norman Panama, Melvin Frank, and James V. Kern. Based on an original story by Everett Freeman and Arthur Schwartz. Songs by Arthur Schwartz and Frank Loesser. Orchestral arrangements by Ray Heindorf. Vocal arrangements by Dudley Chambers. Musical adaptation by Heinz Roemheld. Orchestration: Maurice de Packh. Director of Photography: Arthur Edeson. Dialogue Director: Herbert Farjean. Film Editor: Irene Morra. Art Directors: Anton Grot and Leo K. Kuter. Set Decorator: Walter F. Tilford. Sound: Francis J. Scheid and Charles David Forrest. Gowns: Milo Anderson. Make-up: Perc Westmore. Special Effects: H. F. Koenekamp. Assistant Director: Phil Quinn. Dance numbers created and staged by LeRoy Prinz. Running time: 127 minutes.

CAST
Himself	HUMPHREY BOGART
Himself and *Joe Simpson*	
	EDDIE CANTOR
Herself	BETTE DAVIS
Herself	OLIVIA de HAVILLAND
Himself	ERROL FLYNN
Himself	JOHN GARFIELD
Pat Dixon	JOAN LESLIE
Herself	IDA LUPINO
Tom Randolph	DENNIS MORGAN
Herself	ANN SHERIDAN
Herself	DINAH SHORE
Herself	ALEXIS SMITH
Himself	Jack Carson
Himself	Alan Hale
Himself	George Tobias
Farnsworth	Edward Everett Horton
Dr. Schlenna	S. Z. Sakall
Gossip	Hattie McDaniel
Nurse Hamilton	Ruth Donnelly
Announcer	Don Wilson
Soldier	Willie Best

130

Angelo	Henry Armetta
Girl with a Book	Joyce Reynolds
Barney Jackson	Richard Lane
Dr. Kirby	Paul Harvey
Interne	James Burke
Patient	Bert Gordon
Olaf	Mike Mazurki
Sailor	Frank Faylen

Spike Jones and His City Slickers

Pub Characters in Errol Flynn Number:
Monte Blue, Art Foster, Fred Kelsey, Elmer Ballard, Buster Wiles, Howard Davies, Tudor Williams, Alan Cook, Fred McEvoy, Bobby Hale, Will Stanton, Charles Irwin, David Thursby, Henry Iblings, Earl Hunsaker, Hubert Head, Dudley Kuzelle, Ted Billings

DURING and immediately following World War II, Hollywood put forth several "all-star musicals," each managing to squeeze most of a studio's contract players into songs, dances, sketches, vignettes, or walk-ons. This combination of revue and straight musical, originally popular in the early years of sound, was revived by Paramount with *Star Spangled Rhythm* in 1942. The following year Warners retaliated with *Thank Your Lucky Stars,* the plot construction of which included "a cavalcade of stars benefit for Allied charities."

Flynn, while still appearing at court for the rape trial, contributed a fine song and dance number, "That's What You Jolly Well Get." In this he is a Cockney sailor who wanders into a London pub, where he is obviously known as a fake, and cadges beer with a recital of his exploits in the Pacific, in Lybia, and in the blitz. In mock tribute, the patrons of the pub march him around the premises shoulder high. They sing, "Hurrah, he's won the war," and Flynn rejoins, "and I won the one before." After a few choruses, the group slings him through a window into the street.

A very pointed piece of material, it allowed Flynn to lampoon himself as a war hero. He did it well, and it left a wish that he had been able to do more work like this.

The lyrics of Frank Loesser were suitably matched with a sprightly melody by Arthur Schwartz.

131

Northern Pursuit

With John Ridgely and Helmut Dantine

1943   A Warner Brothers-First National Picture. Directed by Raoul Walsh. Produced by Jack Chertok. Screenplay by Frank Gruber and Alvah Bessie. Based on the story "Five Thousand Trojan Horses" by Leslie T. White. Music by Adolph Deutsch. Director of Photography: Sid Hickox. Dialogue Director: Hugh Cummings. Film Editor: Jack Killifer. Art Director: Leo K. Kuter. Set Decorator: Casey Roberts. Sound: Stanley Jones. Gowns: Leah Rhodes. Make-up: Perc Westmore. Special Effects: E. Roy Davidson. Montages: Don Siegel and James Leicester. Orchestrations: Jerome Moross. Assistant Director: James McMahon. Technical Adviser: Bruce Carruthers. Unit Manager: Lou Baum. Running time: 94 minutes.

CAST
Steve Wagner	ERROL FLYNN
Laura McBain	Julie BISHOP
Colonel Hugo von Keller	
	Helmut DANTINE
Jim Austen	John RIDGELY
Ernst	Gene LOCKHART
Inspector Barnett	Tom Tully
Dagor	Bernard Nedell
Sergeant	Warren Douglas
Jean	Monte Blue
Angus McBain	Alec Craig
Hobby	Tom Fadden
Alice	Rose Higgins
Heinzmann	Richard Alden
German Aviator	John Royce
Indian Guide	Joe Herrera
Radio Operator	Carl Harbaugh
Chief Inspector	Russell Hicks
Colonel	Lester Matthews
Soldier	John Forsythe
Nick the Barber	Charles Judels
Army Driver	James Millican
Guard	Robert Hutton

A FORMULA picture, *Northern Pursuit* presented Flynn as a Canadian Mountie whose

With Tom Tully

With Julie Bishop

parents were born in Germany. He feigns defection from the Mounties and undertakes to guide a party of Nazi saboteurs to their prearranged base in the Hudson Bay region. Flynn's "defection" convinces a number of his compatriots, and even a Nazi contact man (Lockhart). But the party leader (Dantine) plays it safe by forcing Flynn's fiancée (Bishop) to act as hostage on the hazardous journey. Flynn shows his true colors at the finale, when he blocks the Nazis' attempt to take off in a concealed bombing plane.

The idea of a group of Nazis landing in Canada was reminiscent of *The Invaders (49th Parallel),* a 1942 British film which spawned several variations, including Flynn's *Desperate Journey.*

This was Flynn's first picture to be made after the rape trial, and because of its ordinariness and obvious economies, not much of a vote of confidence on the part of his employers.

In one sequence, Flynn is allowed to assure his bride that she is the only girl he ever loved, then turn to the camera with an intimate lift of his eyebrow and confide wonderingly: "What am I saying?"

In May, 1943, while still filming, Flynn collapsed on the set and was hospitalized for about a week. The official release stated that the collapse was due to a "recurrence of an upper respiratory ailment." Every effort was being made by Warners to keep secret Flynn's tuberculosis.

With Julie Bishop, Gene Lockhart,
Helmut Dantine, and Bernard Nedell

133

Uncertain Glory

1944   A Warner Brothers-First National Picture. A Thomson Production. Directed by Raoul Walsh. Produced by Robert Buckner. Screenplay by Laszlo Vadnay and Max Brand. Based on an original story by Joe May and Laszlo Vadnay. Music by Adolph Deutsch. Director of Photography: Sid Hickox. Dialogue Director: James Vincent. Film Editor: George Amy. Art Director: Robert Haas. Set Decorator: Walter F. Tilford. Sound: Oliver S. Garretson. Make-up: Perc Westmore. Special Effects: E. Roy Davidson. Orchestrations: Jerome Moross. Assistant Director: James McMahon. Technical Adviser: Paul Coze. Unit Manager: Frank Mattison. Running time: 102 minutes.

With Faye Emerson

CAST

Jean Picard	ERROL FLYNN	Latour	Victor Kilian
Marcel Bonet	PAUL LUKAS	Saboteur	Ivan Triesault
Marianne	Jean SULLIVAN	Vitrac	Albert Van Antwerp
Mme. Maret	Lucile WATSON	Warden	Art Smith
Louise	Faye Emerson	Innkeeper	Carl Harbaugh
Captain, Mobile Guard	James Flavin	Drover's Wife	Mary Servoss
Police Commissioner	Douglass Dumbrille	Restaurant Keeper	Charles La Torre
Father Le Clerc	Dennis Hoey	Executioner	Pedro de Cordoba
Henri Duval	Sheldon Leonard	Pierre Bonet	Bobby Walberg
Mme. Bonet	Odette Myrtil	Drover	Erskine Sanford
Prison Priest	Francis Pierlot	German Officer	Felix Basch
Razeau	Wallis Clark	Veterinary	Joel Friedkin

With Jean Sullivan and Paul Lukas

With Paul Lukas

UNCERTAIN GLORY was the first picture produced under Flynn's new contract with Warners, an agreement which allowed him considerable say in choice of vehicle, director, and cast, plus a percentage of the profits.

The first choice was a far from good one, for it is badly written, scattered in its development of both narrative and characters, and pedestrian in movement. On its credit side, there is a certain feeling for milieu and mood.

Flynn plays a French criminal who escapes the guillotine during a World War II air raid on Paris. Lukas, a French detective, recaptures him as he heads for Spain. On the way back to Paris their train is rerouted because saboteurs have blown up a bridge, and the two spend some time in a French village, where Flynn has a romantic interlude with a young girl (Sullivan).

The Nazis take one hundred hostages from the village pending the surrender of the saboteur.

Flynn, since he has to die anyway, broaches the idea to Lukas of presenting himself as the saboteur, thus saving the hostages. At first he is merely playing for time, but eventually he decides to do the only redeeming thing in his life, and is executed as the saboteur.

Flynn's characterization was considerably hampered by the script's inconsistencies: depending upon the scene, he is petty and unscrupulous, alert and cunning, stupid and childish, romantic and idealistic, fickle and indulgently sensual.

Flynn and his business manager wanted director Raoul Walsh to go in with them on their set-up to co-produce features with Warners (*Uncertain Glory* being the first.) Walsh declined, as he didn't like some of the less than ethical aspects of the plans. The company—Thomson Productions—was formed with an eye on early liquidation and the taking of a capital gain.

Objective, Burma!

1945 A Warner Brothers-First National Picture. Directed by Raoul Walsh. Produced by Jerry Wald. Screenplay by Ranald Mac-Dougall and Lester Cole. Based on an original story by Alvah Bessie. Music by Franz Waxman. Director of Photography: James Wong Howe. Dialogue Director: John Maxwell. Film Editor: George Amy. Art Director: Ted Smith. Set Decorator: Jack McConaghy. Sound: C. A. Riggs. Make-up: Perc Westmore. Special Effects: Edwin DuPar. Orchestrations: Leonid Raab. Assistant Director: Elmer Decker. Technical Adviser: Major Charles S. Galbraith, US Army Parachute Troops. Unit Manager: Frank Mattison. Running time: 142 minutes.

With William Prince, Warner Anderson, and Frank Tang

CAST	Major Nelson	**ERROL FLYNN**
Sergeant Treacy	James Brown
Lieutenant Jacobs	William Prince
Gabby Gordon	George Tobias
Mark Williams	Henry Hull
Colonel Carter	Warner Anderson
Hogan	John Alvin
Lieutenant Barker	Stephen Richards*
Nebraska Hooper	Richard Erdman
Miggleori	Anthony Caruso
Captain Hennessey	Hugh Beaumont
Negulesco	John Whitney
Brophy	Joel Allen
Soapy Higgins	Buddy Yarus**
Captain Li	Frank Tang
Fred Hollis	William Hudson
Sergeant Chettu	Rodd Redwing
Ghurka	Asit Koomar
Co-Pilot	John Sheridan
Major Fitzpatrick	Lester Matthews
General Stilwell	Erville Anderson

*later known as Mark Stevens
**later known as George Tyne

MOST of the films produced during World War II about the war do not hold up well. *Objective, Burma!* is one of a handful that does.

The fictional plot has Flynn and about three dozen American paratroopers being dropped in a Burmese jungle to find and destroy a Japanese radar station. After accomplishing their mission, the men march through 150 miles of enemy-filled jungle when a plan to get them out by plane fails.

With Henry Hull and George Tyne

A few survivors are rescued when the successful Allied airborne invasion of Burma begins.

A good deal of time and care were obviously put into the film. A better than average script was given a semidocumentary approach and solid, ex-

With Frank Tang, John Alvin, and James Brown

ceptional execution. The Burmese jungle, complete with swamps, was re-created for the most part on the "Lucky" Baldwin Santa Anita ranch near Pasadena and served as convincing background for good jungle warfare detail.

Raoul Walsh's direction and James Wong Howe's photography were remarkable in capturing the operating procedure of the paratroopers, the realistic tensions, the omnipresent danger in the jungles and swamps, the gradual breaking of the men's spirit, and the grim battle scenes.

With Richard Erdman and George Tyne

With Hugh Beaumont, Frank Tang, and Henry Hull

Most of the actors performed with restraint, Flynn being particularly good. None of his occasionally characteristic boyishness, impudent cuteness, or bravura heroics were part of his portrayal. He was straight, professional, and human. The actor regarded the vehicle as one of his few worthwhile works.

Seen today, the film's only negative factors are the usual cross-section of stereotype soldiers, and too much background music, which constantly telegraphs and reinforces the visuals, thereby working against the otherwise splendid documentary approach. However, Franz Waxman did compose an excellent main theme march, the variations of which were most effective when not overused.

After playing a week in a London theater, *Objective, Burma!* was withdrawn because of biased newspaper criticism regarding the film's supposed glorification of America's part in the Burma invasion, and the omission of Britain's major contribution. It was not shown generally in England until 1952, when a new, tactful prologue was added.

San Antonio

1945   A Warner Brothers-First National Picture. Technicolor. Directed by David Butler. Produced by Robert Buckner. Original Screenplay by Alan LeMay and W. R. Burnett. Music by Max Steiner. Director of Photography: Bert Glennon. Dialogue Director: Frederick De Cordova. Film Editor: Irene Morra. Art Director: Ted Smith. Set Decorator: Jack McConaghy. Sound: Everett A. Brown. Wardrobe: Milo Anderson. Make-up: Perc Westmore. Special Effects: Willard Van Enger. Orchestrations: Hugo Friedhofer. Assistant Director: William Kissel. Dance Director: LeRoy Prinz. Color Consultant: Leonard Doss. Running time: 111 minutes.

With Alexis Smith

With Tom Tyler

CAST			
Clay Hardin	ERROL FLYNN	*Sojer Harris*	Charles Stevens
Jeanne Starr	ALEXIS SMITH	*Stagecoach Driver*	Poodles Hanneford
Sacha Bozic	S. Z. Sakall	*Entertainer*	Doodles Weaver
Legare	Victor Francen	*Joey Simms*	Dan White
Henrietta	Florence Bates	*Rebel White*	Ray Spiker
Charley Bell	John Litel	*Hap Winters*	Al Hill
Roy Stuart	Paul Kelly	*Hawker*	Harry Cording
Captain Morgan	Robert Shayne	*Poker Player*	Chalky Williams
Pony Smith	John Alvin	*Tip Brice*	Wallis Clark
Cleve Andrews	Monte Blue	*Roper*	Bill Steele
Colonel Johnson	Robert Barrat	*Henchman*	Allen E. Smith
Ricardo Torreon	Pedro de Cordoba	*Henchman*	Howard Hill
Lafe McWilliams	Tom Tyler	*Specialty Dancer*	Arnold Kent
Hymie Rosas	Chris-Pin Martin	*Laredo Border Guard*	Dan Seymour

With Robert Shayne, Paul Kelly, Monte Blue, Victor Francen, Pedro de Cordoba, S. Z. Sakall, and Alexis Smith

142

With Victor Francen

AS Flynn's first Western since *They Died with Their Boots On* four years earlier, *San Antonio* is perfunctory from most standpoints. It contains an artificially staged saloon brawl (not up to the one in *Dodge City),* a final gunfight within the hallowed walls of the Alamo, and an interesting mixed bag of supporting players who seem disparate and out of their element, and who are unable to take the curse off the uninspired script.

The story concerns an 1877 cattleman (Flynn) who returns to San Antonio from Mexico, where he has obtained proof that the owner of San Antonio's leading dance hall (Kelly) is the head of a well-organized syndicate of cattle thieves. Flynn suspects a New York actress (Smith), who has come to sing at the dance hall, of being in league with the rustlers. Naturally, Flynn has trouble convicting Kelly, but it all works out at the finale.

During her tenure at the saloon, as a kind of musical-comedy relief, Alexis is seen rendering several choruses of two songs, and near the beginning of the film, she and Errol engage in a bit of Mexican-style dancing.

Warners' Calabasas Ranch, about twenty miles from the Burbank lot, was the scene of most of the exterior action.

Pressed into reuse was Max Steiner's main title music from *Dodge City*. It worked equally well behind *San Antonio*'s main title.

By no means a Western type, Flynn was the only non-American actor to become successful in this kind of film in the United States. He confessed to being baffled by this success, and referred to himself as the "rich man's Roy Rogers." By the time he made *San Antonio* Flynn had surrendered himself, and obviously decided to enjoy the nonsense along with the customers.

With Paul Kelly and Victor Francen

Never Say Goodbye

1946   A Warner Brothers-First National Picture. Directed by James V. Kern. Produced by William Jacobs. Screenplay by I. A. L. Diamond and James V. Kern. Adaptation by Lewis R. Foster. Based on an original story by Ben and Norma Barzman. Music by Frederick Hollander. Director of Photography: Arthur Edeson. Dialogue Director: Robert Stevens. Film Editor: Folmar Blangsted. Art Director: Anton Grot. Set Decorator: Budd Friend. Sound: Stanley Jones. Wardrobe: Leah Rhodes. Make-up: Perc Westmore. Special Effects: William McGann and Willard Van Enger. Orchestrations: Leonid Raab. Assistant Director: Phil Quinn. Unit Manager: Don Page. Paintings and sketches by Miss Zoe Mozert. Running time: 97 minutes.

CAST   *Phil Gayley*   ERROL FLYNN
       Ellen Gayley   ELEANOR PARKER
       Phillippa (Flip) Gayley   Patti Brady
       Mrs. Hamilton   Lucile Watson
       Luigi   S. Z. Sakall
       Corporal Fenwick Lonkowski
                                  Forrest Tucker
       Rex DeVallon   Donald Woods
       Nancy Graham   Peggy Knudsen
       Jack Gordon   Tom D'Andrea
       Cozy   Hattie McDaniel
       Withers   Charles Coleman
       McCarthy   Arthur Shields
       Policeman   Tom Tyler
       Policeman   Monte Blue

With Peggy Knudsen, Harry Hays Morgan, and S. Z. Sakall

144

With Eleanor Parker

IT took five writers to concoct this rehash of tired plot machinations, time-worn gags, and padded situations. The basic story is that old chestnut about the divorced couple who are still in love, and are being held together by their seven-year-old daughter.

Among other things, the unraveling includes the bit about the child who started writing letters to a Marine overseas, and how he came back and mistook her mother for the correspondent (courtesy of *Dear Ruth,* etc.). There's the routine about how the little girl asks for a pair of brothers with whom to play, whereupon Daddy coyly mentions two names and thereby creates imaginary playmates. There is the restaurant mixup with Flynn trying to juggle two dinner dates—in separate rooms—with neither young lady knowing of the other's presence until the end of the sequence.

Another bit of padding to prolong the inevitable conclusion is the fake mirror bit, with Flynn in a Santa Claus outfit, mimicking Donald Woods in a Santa Claus outfit, who thinks he is looking into a mirror.

The script also allowed Flynn to sing a few bars of the song "Remember Me" and do an imitation of Humphrey Bogart—greatly aided by the dubbed-in voice of Bogart himself.

Flynn also was presented as being considerably less than a tough guy. In one sequence his daughter bursts into laughter when Dad threatens to "tear apart" her mother's Marine admirer (Tucker). Flynn looks at her wistfully and asks, "Well, you believed in me as Robin Hood, didn't you?" "Yes," she answers, "but that was just make-believe."

With Lucile Watson, Donald Woods, Eleanor Parker, and Patti Brady

145

Cry Wolf

1947 A Warner Brothers-First National Picture. A Thomson Production. Directed by Peter Godfrey. Produced by Henry Blanke. Screenplay by Catherine Turney. Based on the novel by Marjorie Carleton. Music by Franz Waxman. Director of Photography: Carl Guthrie. Dialogue Director: Felix Jacoves. Film Editor: Folmar Blangsted. Art Director: Carl Jules Weyl. Set Decorator: Jack McConaghy. Sound: Charles Lang. Wardrobe: Travilla. Miss Stanwyck's Wardrobe: Edith Head. Make-up: Perc Westmore. Special Effects: William McGann and Robert Burks. Orchestrations: Leonid Raab. Assistant Director: Claude Archer. Unit Manager: Don Page. Running time: 83 minutes.

With Barbara Stanwyck

CAST

Mark Caldwell	ERROL FLYNN
Sandra Marshall	
	BARBARA STANWYCK
Julie Demarest	Geraldine BROOKS
James Demarest	Richard BASEHART
Senator Caldwell	Jerome COWAN
Jackson Laidell	John Ridgely
Angela	Patricia White
Becket	Rory Mallinson
Marta	Helene Thimig
Davenport	Paul Stanton
Roberts	Barry Bernard
Clergyman	John Elliott
Mrs. Laidell	Lisa Golm
Watkins	Jack Mower
Gatekeeper	Paul Panzer
Dr. Reynolds	Creighton Hale

*With Barbara Stanwyck and
Geraldine Brooks*

IN the opening scene of one of the least typical of Flynn's vehicles, a widow (Stanwyck) arrives at the house of mourning much to the surprise of the family, who didn't know the deceased was married. She soon reveals that this had been a recent marriage of convenience to help the young man get his inheritance held by Uncle Mark (Flynn), and it was to be followed by divorce in six months.

Uncle Mark is suspicious of the woman, and she has cause to be suspicious of him. He turns out to be something of a scientist with a laboratory in an unused wing of the house. The widow decides to snoop about and find out what secrets the mysterious mausoleum-like house is keeping.

She eventually finds her presumed-dead husband (Basehart) wandering about the grounds.

He tries to kill Mark, and demonstrates, before accidentally dying, the streak of family insanity from which Mark in his devious, harsh manner has been trying to shield the widow.

Dour, leering servants, an hysterical niece who commits suicide (Brooks), and weird noises in the night, are additional components of the puzzling ingredients.

Flynn underplays in a properly sinister, stuffy, and apparently sadistic manner, but in some scenes he is too wooden.

An excellent Franz Waxman score tries valiantly to support the melodramatics, but the conjured mood and suspense are negated by unsatisfactory dialogue and a plot that does not quite work.

*With John Ridgely and
Barbara Stanwyck*

Escape Me Never

1947   A Warner Brothers-First National Picture. Directed by Peter Godfrey. Produced by Henry Blanke. Screenplay by Thames Williamson. Based on the novel *The Fool of the Family,* and the play *Escape Me Never* by Margaret Kennedy. Music by Erich Wolfgang Korngold. Director of Photography: Sol Polito. Dialogue Director: Robert Stevens. Ballet sequences staged and directed by LeRoy Prinz. Film Editor: Clarence Kolster. Art Director: Carl Jules Weyl. Set Decorator: Fred M. MacLean. Sound: Dolph Thomas. Wardrobe: Bernard Newman. Ballet Costumes: Travilla. Make-up: Perc Westmore. Special Effects: Harry Barndollar and Willard Van Enger. Orchestrations: Hugo Friedhofer and Ray Heindorf. Assistant Director: Claude Archer. Unit Manager: Al Alleborn. Running time: 104 minutes.

CAST

Sebastian Dubrok	ERROL FLYNN
Gemma Smith	IDA LUPINO
Fenella MacLean	ELEANOR PARKER
Caryl Dubrok	GIG YOUNG
Ivor MacLean	Reginald Denny
Mrs. MacLean	Isobel Elsom
Professor Heinrich	Albert Basserman
Mr. Steinach	Ludwig Stossel
Natrova	Milada Mladova
Dancer	George Zoritch
Landlady	Helene Thimig
Guide	Frank Puglia
Minister	Frank Reicher
Mrs. Cooper	Doris Lloyd
Dino	Anthony Caruso
Choreographer	Ivan Triesault

With Eleanor Parker

With Ida Lupino

THE CONSTANT NYMPH, a Warner film originally slated for Flynn but eventually made with Charles Boyer, was one of 1943's biggest hits. Another story, and a kind of sequel by the same author, Margaret Kennedy, similar in mood, style, and outlook, was planned as a follow-up and completed in February, 1946, but not released until almost two years later. *Escape Me*

With Eleanor Parker and Gig Young

With Frank Reicher and Ida Lupino

Never, a remake of the 1935 British film, remained true to its even then old-fashioned, sentimental origins.

The story starts with a young heiress (Parker) suspecting her fiancé (Young) of being involved with a young mother (Lupino). Actually it's the fiancé's brother (Flynn), an impoverished musician, who is housing the waif and her baby. To correct the misunderstanding, the trio plus baby follow the lady of means into the Alps to explain the situation, only to have Flynn fall in love with her. After much consternation, he agrees to marry Lupino and then goes off to England to write a ballet inspired by Miss Parker. Later, Flynn becomes involved with the heiress again, but on the night he goes away with her his wife's baby dies. At this critical moment the composer decides against infidelity, changes the name of the ballet in honor of his wife, and all concludes happily on opening night.

None of this played too well, and the production suffered from the use of obvious process shots and sound-stage simulations of the Alps and other exterior settings that were largely unbelievable.

Flynn was not at his best attempting to portray a musical genius, although, despite the script and direction, he did do quite well in a few isolated scenes. Hugh Sinclair played his role in the first version and Elisabeth Bergner originated Lupino's character.

Erich Korngold's music was by far the best thing about the film. His first picture with Flynn since *The Sea Hawk,* it was also to be his last with the actor. In addition to the general excellence of the score, Korngold wrote for the film a short original ballet, *Primavera,* and a popular song that was well received, "Love for Love."

Silver River

1948   A Warner Brothers-First National Picture. Directed by Raoul Walsh. Produced by Owen Crump. Screenplay by Stephen Longstreet and Harriet Frank, Jr. Based on an unpublished novel by Stephen Longstreet. Music by Max Steiner. Director of Photography: Sid Hickox. Film Editor: Alan Crosland, Jr. Art Director: Ted Smith. Set Decorator: William G. Wallace. Sound: Francis J. Scheid. Ann Sheridan's Wardrobe: Travilla. Men's Wardrobe: Marjorie Best. Make-up: Perc Westmore. Special Effects: William McGann and Edwin DuPar. Montages: James Leicester. Orchestrations: Murray Cutter. Assistant Director: Russell Saunders. Technical Adviser on Civil War sequences: Colonel J. G. Taylor, US Army, Retired. Unit Manager: Chuck Hansen. Running time: 110 minutes.

CAST		
Mike McComb	ERROL FLYNN	
Georgia Moore	ANN SHERIDAN	
John Plato Beck	Thomas MITCHELL	
Stanley Moore	Bruce BENNETT	
Pistol Porter	Tom D'Andrea	
Banjo Sweeney	Barton MacLane	
Buck Chevigee	Monte Blue	
Major Spencer	Jonathan Hale	
Sam Slade	Alan Bridge	
Major Ross	Arthur Space	
Major Wilson	Art Baker	
President Grant	Joseph Crehan	

With Tom D'Andrea and Jonathan Hale

With Monte Blue, Ann Sheridan, and Harry Woods

With Barton MacLane, Tom D'Andrea, and Harry Woods

SILVER RIVER opens with some well-staged and exciting Civil War battle scenes, then has Flynn being cashiered from the Union Army to later become an unscrupulous gambler. Up to this point, the film shows remarkable promise, but when Flynn manages to muscle into the silver mining game, eventually becoming an undisputed power in the West, the pace slackens, and a nineteenth-century variation of the biblical tale of King David, Bathsheba, and Uriah unfolds, with a new twist at the end. Sending his lieutenant (Bennett) into a death trap, Flynn then marries his widow (Sheridan), and after she has had enough of his ruthlessness and leaves him, he sees the light and reforms.

Flynn portrayed the reprobate protagonist quite well (in some ways a forerunner of his Soames Forsyte in *That Forsyte Woman),* and it is too bad that the script didn't deliver more than routine construction and dialogue after the first two or three reels. It is a good performance wasted on a disappointing film.

The exteriors were shot at Calabasas, the Sierras above Bishop, and in Hollywood's Bronson Canyon.

This was Raoul Walsh's last picture with Flynn. The veteran director had been with the swashbuckler on seven pictures commencing with *They Died with Their Boots On* in 1941, and the two had become close friends (Flynn called Walsh "Uncle"). Walsh was able to control Flynn on most of their earlier films. It took a hard disciplinarian to get the best out of the actor—particularly when he wasn't interested in the film—and Walsh qualified. He made a deal with Flynn: no liquor during shooting until 5:00 P.M. According to Walsh, if the actor stuck to this bargain, then the director would join him in imbibing after that hour. But, by the time *Silver River* was made, Flynn had spent three years with softer directors. He and Walsh never worked together again after the completion of *Silver River.*

With Thomas Mitchell

With Ann Sheridan and Thomas Mitchell

Adventures of Don Juan

1949 A Warner Brothers-First National Picture. Directed by Vincent Sherman. Produced by Jerry Wald. Screenplay by George Oppenheimer and Harry Kurnitz. Based on an original story by Herbert Dalmas. Music by Max Steiner. Director of Photography: Elwood Bredell. Dialogue Director: Maurice Murphy. Film Editor: Alan Crosland, Jr. Art Director: Edward Carrere. Set Decorator: Lyle B. Reifsnider. Sound: Everett A. Brown. Costumes: Leah Rhodes, Travilla, and Marjorie Best. Make-up: Perc Westmore. Special Effects: William McGann and John Crouse. Orchestrations: Murray Cutter. Assistant Director: Richard Mayberry. Fencing Master: Fred Cavens. Color Consultant: Mitchell Kovaleski. Unit Manager: Frank Mattison. Running time: 110 minutes.

CAST

Don Juan de Marana	ERROL FLYNN
Queen Margaret	VIVECA LINDFORS
Duke de Lorca	Robert DOUGLAS
Leporello	Alan HALE
King Philip III	Romney Brent
Donna Elena	Ann Rutherford
Count de Polan	Robert Warwick
Don Sebastian	Jerry Austin
Don Rodrigo	Douglas Kennedy
Donna Carlotta	Jeanne Shepherd
Catherine	Mary Stuart
Lady Diana	Helen Westcott
Don Serafino	Fortunio Bonanova
Lord Chalmers	Aubrey Mather
Duenna	Una O'Connor
Captain Alvarez	Raymond Burr
Catherine's Husband	G. P. Huntley, Jr.
Innkeeper	David Leonard
Don de Cordoba	Leon Belasco
Pachecho	Pedro de Cordoba
Count D'Orsini	David Bruce
Turnkey	Monte Blue
Innkeeper's Daughter	Barbara Bates
Innkeeper's Son	Harry Lewis

FOLLOWING the 1943 rape trial, the public became considerably interested in Flynn's off-screen exploits—most of the more colorful ones making the press. His various amours, brawls, alimony problems, and drinking escapades were duly reported and helped to create a shift in his screen portrayals. The characters he played in the mid and late 1940s contained at least a hint of the roué or libertine, and on occasion he even ap-

With Aubrey Mather and
Helen Westcott

With Viveca Lindfors

155

Warners had made a silent *Don Juan* in 1926 with John Barrymore, and since certain parallels between the legendary Don Juan character and Barrymore/Flynn were obvious, the choice seemed logical.

Originally scheduled to commence shooting in May, 1945, under Raoul Walsh's direction, *Adventures of Don Juan* had a long and disruptive history before it finally reached theaters. Because of a lengthy jurisdictional union dispute involving studio set designers, the original starting date was canceled, as few sets were being constructed during the resulting industry-wide strike.

Over the next two and a half years, the project was reactivated on different occasions, but never got off the ground. Meanwhile there were dissatisfactions with the script, and producer Jerry Wald had a score of writers revising and embellishing the original story-line. At one point "Max Brand" (Frederick Faust) did a draft, and on another occasion William Faulkner contributed a version.

Finally, shooting started in October, 1947, but after a few weeks Flynn took off and left town for weeks on a major binge. The company shut down and resumed some time later, but Flynn was still a problem. He started showing the effects from drinking in mid-afternoon, necessitating a good deal of shooting around him. Also, he could not sustain a scene for long, so *Don Juan* was artfully assembled from bits and pieces of more than the usual number of camera set-ups and takes, according to director Vincent Sherman. Lighting and make-up were carefully utilized to hide the

peared as a distinctly unpleasant and/or ruthless person.

In 1944, when there was a major interest in diverting historical-romantic fiction, Jack Warner decided to put Flynn back in a big-budget swashbuckler. But rather than the youthful, brimming-with-virtue hero, the new protagonist would be more world-weary, fickle, wry, and a distinct ladies' man—but still dashing, with sword and horse. A Don Juan, so to speak.

With Robert Douglas

somewhat debauched features of the once perfect face; but even with this care it was obvious that the actor was not in his prime. Still, Flynn's performance on screen was, and is quite good.

Don Juan had become a nervous enterprise; the film had gone considerably over the $2 million budget. Also, 1947 saw a major decline in box-office receipts—a marked contrast to the lush World War II years. So some reworking of the script to save money took place. A major sequence involving a great ball was eliminated. Another lengthy scene near the beginning of the picture was built entirely around stock footage of Essex' triumphant victory parade on his return from Cadiz, courtesy of *Elizabeth and Essex*. Bits and pieces showing Robin of Locksley's escape from Nottingham Castle in *Robin Hood* also were cut in.

Don Juan, in spite of everything, emerged as a good film. If it is not quite in the same league with *Robin Hood* or *The Sea Hawk,* there are compensating factors: fine Technicolor photography, a lush, complementary Max Steiner score (Korngold was originally set, but by the time the film was completed, he had left Warners), first-rate dueling sequences, and one truly magnificent set representing a huge staircase in the king's palace, upon which the stirring and stylish duel-to-the-death between Flynn and villain Robert Douglas takes place. The final action sequences in a torture chamber, in the halls of the palace, and on the grand staircase are among the best of their kind. Incidentally, Don Juan's spectacular

With Viveca Lindfors

leap down the stairs onto his opponent was actually performed by Jock Mahoney, the only stunt man willing to undertake such a difficult stunt.

This version of the Don Juan legend owes little or nothing to any preceding Don Juan in drama, literature, poetry, or music. Nor did it utilize the Barrymore story-line involving the great lover with the Borgias in Italy. Much of the Flynn version had to do with a somewhat reformed Juan saving lovely Queen Margaret of seventeenth-century Spain (portrayed by Sweden's Viveca Lindfors,

With Alan Hale, Jerry Austin, and Ann Rutherford

157

who had recently been imported by Warners) and her slightly addled king, Philip III (Brent) from the evil machinations of the king's fictional minister, the Duke de Lorca (Douglas). Originally, in 1945, George Coulouris was to play the duke.

The early portions of the narrative showing Juan's balcony climbings, wooings, and encounters with irate husbands were lighthearted, satirical, and rather witty: a spoof of the character and of Flynn himself.

The film opens with this scene: It is evening and Juan has climbed the moonlit balcony of an eager young lady. He greets her, takes her in his arms, and, filled with quiet yet intense ardor, says: "I have loved you since the beginning of time."

His paramour responds, "But you only met me yesterday."

"That was when time began," Juan replies, without hesitation.

The lady speaks a mild reproach: "But you've made love to so many women."

And Juan draws an inspired analogy: "Catherine, an artist may paint a thousand canvases

With Robert Douglas

158

before achieving one work of art—would you deny a lover the same practice?"

Later, he is interrupted in a prelude to amour by a returning bridegroom-to-be who draws his sword and cries out: "You're caught!"

Juan wearily replies, "The story of my life."

Once he meets Queen Margaret—Juan's eventual true love—and becomes involved in court intrigue, an alternating melodramatic and sentimental air prevails. Except for the epilogue: Juan, having given up the queen to her regal duties, foreswears love and is about to devote his life to scholarly pursuits. A coach passes bearing a lovely and beckoning lady. In a flash, he starts to pursue her, saying to his faithful servant, Leporello (Hale): "There is a little bit of Don Juan in every man, but since I am Don Juan, there must be more of it in me!"

Nora Eddington (Flynn's second wife) appeared briefly as the lady in the coach.

Although extremely successful in Europe, *Don Juan* did only reasonably well in U.S. theaters—certainly nothing commensurate with its headaches and cost. It was evident that the Flynn golden days were not going to have a renaissance. But, ironically, both *The Sea Hawk* and *Robin Hood* were nationally reissued while *Don Juan* was being prepared, shot, and edited, and both did exceptionally well.

Following, and as a result of, *Don Juan,* the budgets on Flynn's remaining Warner films were drastically reduced.

*With Alan Hale and
Nora Eddington*

159

It's a
Great Feeling

1949 A Warner Brothers-First National Picture. Technicolor. Directed by David Butler. Produced by Alex Gottlieb. Screenplay by Jack Rose and Melville Shavelson. Based on an original story by I. A. L. Diamond. Songs by Jule Styne and Sammy Cahn. Musical Direction and Incidental Score by Ray Heindorf. Musical Numbers Staged and Directed by LeRoy Prinz. Director of Photography: Wilfrid M. Cline. Dialogue Director: Herschel Daugherty. Film Editor: Irene Morra. Art Director: Stanley Fleischer. Set Decorator: Lyle B. Reifsnider. Sound: Dolph Thomas and Charles David Forrest. Wardrobe: Milo Anderson. Make-up: Perc Westmore. Special Effects: William McGann and H. F. Koenekamp. Orchestrations: Leo Shuken and Sidney Cutner. Assistant Director: Phil Quinn. Color Consultant: Mitchell Kovaleski. Unit Manager: Frank Mattison. Running time: 85 minutes.

CAST		
Himself	DENNIS MORGAN
Judy Adams	DORIS DAY
Himself	JACK CARSON
Arthur Trent	Bill Goodwin
Information Clerk	Irving Bacon
Grace	Claire Carleton
Publicity Man	Harlan Warde
Trent's Secretary	Jacqueline DeWitt

The Mazzone-Abbott Dancers

Himself	David Butler
Himself	Michael Curtiz
Himself	King Vidor
Himself	Raoul Walsh

Guest Stars

Himself	GARY COOPER
Herself	JOAN CRAWFORD
Jeffrey Bushdinkel	ERROL FLYNN
Himself	SYDNEY GREENSTREET
Himself	DANNY KAYE
Herself	PATRICIA NEAL
Herself	ELEANOR PARKER
Himself	RONALD REAGAN
Himself	EDWARD G. ROBINSON
Herself	JANE WYMAN

THIS behind-the-scenes Hollywood musical included guest appearances by several of Warners' stars and directors.

Morgan and Carson, playing themselves, are presented as having great difficulties in securing a director for their forthcoming picture, due to Carson's colossal ego and "ham" tendencies. After Carson takes over the directorial reigns himself, the team then has the same problem in engaging a female lead; so they discover Doris, who has been working as a waitress in the studio commissary. Later, she becomes disenchanted during production, returns home to Wisconsin, and in the last thirty seconds marries her old boy friend, who is revealed to be Flynn.

Much of the film takes place on the Warner lot, but as a spoof and satire on Hollywood, it is only sporadically funny.

That Forsyte Woman

1949   Metro-Goldwyn-Mayer Picture. Technicolor. Directed by Compton Bennett. Produced by Leon Gordon. Screenplay by Jan Lustig, Ivan Tors, and James B. Williams. Additional dialogue by Arthur Wimperis. Based on the novel *The Man of Property* (Book One of *The Forsyte Saga*) by John Galsworthy. Music by Bronislau Kaper. Director of Photography: Joseph Ruttenberg. Film Editor: Frederick Y. Smith. Art Directors: Cedric Gibbons and Daniel B. Cathcart. Set Decorators: Edwin B. Willis and Jack D. Moore. Sound: Douglas Shearer and Ralph Pender. Women's Costumes: Walter Plunkett. Men's Costumes: Valles. Make-up: Jack Dawn. Hair Styles: Sydney Guilaroff. Assistant Director: Robert Barnes. Color Consultants: Henri Jaffa and James Gooch. Unit Manager: Hugh Bosewell. Running time: 114 minutes.

CAST *Soames Forsyte*   ERROL FLYNN

Irene Forsyte	GREER GARSON
Young Jolyon Forsyte	
	WALTER PIDGEON
Philip Bosinney	ROBERT YOUNG
June Forsyte	Janet LEIGH
Old Jolyon Forsyte	Harry Davenport
James Forsyte	Aubrey Mather
Beveridge	Gerald Oliver Smith
Roger Forsyte	Lumsden Hare
Swithin Forsyte	Stanley Logan
Nicholas Forsyte	Halliwell Hobbes
Timothy Forsyte	Matt Moore
Ann Forsyte Hayman	Florence Auer
Julia Forsyte Small	Phyllis Morris
Hester Forsyte	Marjorie Eaton
Mrs. Taylor	Evelyn Beresford
Chester Forsyte	Richard Lupino
Dric Forsyte	Wilson Wood
Alice Forsyte	Constance Cavendish
Mrs. Winthrop	Isabel Randolph
Mr. McLean	Reginald Sheffield
Director Braval	Andre Charlot
Lord Dunstable	Frank Baker
Porter	Billy Bevan

Galsworthy's lengthy trilogy, *The Forsyte Saga*. This was Flynn's first picture away from the Warner studio.

Flynn played Soames Forsyte, pillar of society, cornerstone of convention, and typical upper-middle-class "man of property" in the Victorian era. The story attempts to develop the struggle between the ideas symbolized by Soames, who merely possesses, but is incapable of giving completely of himself to anyone or anything, and Irene, his wife (Garson), who represents a "modern" woman, a rebel against ownership, and a free spirit. Irene falls in love with a young architect (Young), who also is against convention, but is too impulsive and romantic. After the architect dies, Irene leaves Soames and marries the black sheep artist of the Forsyte family, Soames's prosaic cousin (Pidgeon), who embodies all the "best" qualities of the Bohemian soul and the practical man. Soames is left with a flock of possessions, but still, presumably, without a heart.

IN November of 1947, Flynn signed a new contract with Warners allowing him to do one outside picture a year. In late 1948 he was loaned to MGM, in exchange for William Powell's services in *Life with Father,* to appear with Greer Garson in an adaptation of the first part of John

With Janet Leigh, Robert Young, and Greer Garson

The action of the film antedates the opening of Book One of the *Saga*. As the novel begins, Irene and Soames are already married. The film goes back to show why Soames was attracted to Irene and how he won her for his wife.

Originally Flynn was to play the Pidgeon or Robert Young role, but he insisted on tackling Soames. In this instance he exercised good judgment. Jolyon, the Bohemian, or Bosinney, the architect, would have been a watered-down version of Flynn's part in *Escape Me Never,* which in itself was not much.

That Forsyte Woman unfortunately is pretty dull going, but it did contain the kernel of what could have been an outstanding performance for Flynn. He captures all of the pomp, stuffiness, and frustrations of the character in a first-rate manner. Due to the script and direction, however, he seems more unpleasant than Galsworthy intended, perhaps to justify the fickle behavior of Garson's character. One can see that Flynn tries hard, and was capable of projecting more complexity and subtleness into Soames, but the general treatment thwarted him. However, Flynn regarded the role as one of his favorites, and behaved responsibly on the MGM lot, according to Greer Garson and others present at the time.

With Walter Pidgeon

With Greer Garson

Miss Garson recently recalled that Flynn "presented out of his artistic and creative imagination, with no assistance from anybody else, a believable and most interesting portrait of Soames Forsyte; so completely different from anything else that he had done that it made one realize what potential he had as an actor."

Director Compton Bennett, on the strength of one British film, *The Seventh Veil,* was given this assignment in Hollywood.

With Greer Garson and Charles McNaughton

With Alexis Smith

Montana

1950 A Warner Brothers-First National Picture. Technicolor. Directed by Ray Enright. Produced by William Jacobs. Screenplay by James R. Webb, Borden Chase, and Charles O'Neal. Based on an original story by Ernest Haycox. Music by David Buttolph. Director of Photography: Karl Freund. Dialogue Director: Gene Lewis. Film Editor: Frederick Richards. Art Director: Charles H. Clarke. Set Decorator: G. W. Berntsen. Sound: Francis J. Scheid. Wardrobe: Milo Anderson. Flynn's Wardrobe: Marjorie Best. Make-up: Perc Westmore. Orchestrations: Leo Shuken and Sidney Cutner. Assistant Director: Oren Haglund. Color Consultant: William Fritzsche. Unit Manager: Lou Baum. Song "Reckon I'm in Love" by Mack David, Al Hoffman, and Jerry Livingston. Running time: 76 minutes.

CAST

Morgan Lane	ERROL FLYNN
Maria Singleton	ALEXIS SMITH
Poppa Schultz	S. Z. Sakall
Rodney Ackroyd	Douglas Kennedy
Tex Coyne	James Brown
Slim Reeves	Ian MacDonald
MacKenzie	Charles Irwin
Tecumseh Burke	Paul E. Burns
Jock	Tudor Owen
George Forsythe	Lester Matthews
Pedro	Nacho Galindo
Jake Overby	Lane Chandler
Charlie Penrose	Monte Blue
Baker	Billy Vincent
Curley Bennett	Warren Jackson

With Paul E. Burns and Ian MacDonald

With Alexis Smith

AFTER *They Died with Their Boots On,* Flynn's Westerns were considerably less than epic. The vigor, the splendor, the outstanding action sequences of the earlier films were only hinted at in subsequent efforts. *Montana,* the least impressive of the group, was a formula film (running a scant one hour and sixteen minutes), with a dull, undistinguished script. The scenery (Warners' Calabasas Ranch) was well photographed, the production was reasonably well mounted, but the people and situations were devoid of life and interest.

Flynn, relying almost completely on debonair charm to see him through the tedium, plays an Australian sheepherder determined to move in on the cattle territory of Montana. Alexis, as a wealthy cattle rancher opposed to any invasion of sheepherders, is attracted to Flynn before she realizes his true occupation. But once the truth is out, it's Errol and his sheepherders versus Alexis and the cattle barons. Fortunately, at the conclusion, Errol and Alexis, cattle and sheep—all get together.

Flynn sang for the fourth time on the screen: a little ditty called "Reckon I'm in Love." This was a duet with Alexis, accompanied by what appears to be Flynn's guitar playing. He had sung a few bars of a Mexican folk ballad in *San Antonio,* also accompanying himself on the guitar.

Montana is one of two films in which Flynn portrayed an Australian, his true nationality; the other being *Desperate Journey.*

Rocky Mountain

1950 A Warner Brothers-First National Picture. Directed by William Keighley. Produced by William Jacobs. Screenplay by Winston Miller and Alan LeMay. Based on an original story by Alan LeMay. Music by Max Steiner. Director of Photography: Ted McCord. Film Editor: Rudi Fehr. Art Director: Stanley Fleischer. Set Decorator: L. S. Edwards. Sound: Stanley Jones. Wardrobe: Marjorie Best. Orchestrations: Murray Cutter. Assistant Director: Frank Mattison. Running time: 83 minutes.

CAST		
Lafe Barstow	ERROL FLYNN	
Johanna Carter	Patrice WYMORE	
Lieutenant Rickey	Scott FORBES	
Pap Dennison		
	Guinn (Big Boy) WILLIAMS	
Jim Wheat	Dick Jones	
Cole Smith	Howard Petrie	
Plank	Slim Pickens	
Gil Craigie	Chubby Johnson	
Kip Waterson	Buzz Henry	
Kay Rawlins	Sheb Wooley	
Pierre Duchesne	Peter Coe	
Jonas Weatherby	Rush Williams	
Ash	Steve Dunhill	
Barnes	Alex Sharp	
Ryan	Yakima Canutt	
Man Dog	Nakai Snez	

With Scott Forbes and Patrice Wymore

167

With Chubby Johnson, Guinn (Big Boy) Williams, Dick Jones, Peter Coe, and Buzz Henry

ROCKY MOUNTAIN's assets are the splendid location sites near Gallup, New Mexico, where the entire picture was interestingly photographed, the well-staged Indian attack on a stagecoach, and the final chase and battle between a small group of Confederate soldiers and a tribe of Indians. The Indians were Navajos recruited from the surrounding location area.

The story, based on a true incident, had possibilities, but the script was just average and filled with the usual cross-section of superficial characters.

In his last Western, Flynn played, in a straight and convincing manner, a Confederate officer traveling with a small band of men in California on orders to persuade outlaws to join their group

With Patrice Wymore

168

With Howard Petrie, Peter Coe,
Buzz Henry, Sheb Wooley, and Slim
Pickens. In front row: Dick Jones,
Guinn (Big Boy) Williams, and
Rush Williams.

and thus hopefully control the West for the Confederacy.

They save a girl in a stagecoach (Wymore) from an Indian attack. She was on her way to join her fiancé, an officer in the Union Army (Forbes). Flynn and his men later succeed in capturing a Yankee patrol with the fiancé in command. After a series of complications, the Yankees escape, but the Confederates, in order to save the girl, divert attacking Indians and are massacred.

While on location, Flynn became interested in the woman who was to become his third wife, Warner contract player Patrice Wymore. She had appeared in only one previous film, *Tea for Two.* Her thankless part in *Rocky Mountain* did little for her as an actress, but she looked pretty and moved with a dancer's grace.

169

Kim

1951 A Metro-Goldwyn-Mayer Picture. Technicolor. Directed by Victor Saville. Produced by Leon Gordon. Screenplay by Leon Gordon, Helen Deutsch, and Richard Schayer. Based on the novel by Rudyard Kipling. Music by André Previn. Director of Photography: William V. Skall. Film Editor: George Boemler. Art Directors: Cedric Gibbons and Hans Peters. Set Decorators: Edwin B. Willis, Arthur Krams, and Hugh Hunt. Sound: Douglas Shearer and Standish Lambert. Costumes: Valles. Make-up: William Tuttle and Ben Lane. Hair Styles: Sydney Guilaroff. Special Effects: A. Arnold Gillespie and Warren Newcombe. Montage sequence: Peter Ballbusch. Assistant Director: George Rhein. Technical Adviser: I. A. Hafesjee. Color Consultants: Henri Jaffa and James Gooch. Unit Manager: Keith Weeks. Running time: 113 minutes.

CAST

Mahbub Ali, the Red Beard	
	ERROL FLYNN
Kim	Dean STOCKWELL
Lama	Paul LUKAS
Colonel Creighton	Robert DOUGLAS
Emissary	Thomas Gomez
Hurree Chunder	Cecil Kellaway
Lurgan Sahib	Arnold Moss
Father Victor	Reginald Owen
Laluli	Laurette Luez
Hassan Bey	Richard Hale
The Russians	{ Roman Toporow { Ivan Triesault
Major Ainsley	Hayden Rorke
Dr. Bronson	Walter Kingsford
Shadow	Frank Lackteen
Foster Mother	Jeanette Nolan

AFTER *That Forsyte Woman,* Flynn was announced for another MGM film, *King Solomon's Mines,* to be filmed for the most part in

With Dean Stockwell

Africa. Eventually, Stewart Granger played the white hunter in that excellent film, while Flynn shifted to *Kim,* some of which was shot in India at the same time the *Mines* troupe was in Africa. Unfortunately, Flynn, or someone advising him, made the wrong choice between the two projects.

Kim had been sitting around Metro for some time. In 1938 it was announced as a vehicle to be produced in India with Freddie Bartholomew and Robert Taylor. World War II shut the project down. In 1942 it was reactivated as a Hollywood-based production to feature Mickey Rooney, Conrad Veidt, and Basil Rathbone. This too was shelved at the suggestion of the Office of War Information, who feared that the Orient might be offended by the book's implications of white supremacy and imperialism.

In 1948 the new Indian government, apparently having decided that British imperialism was now just a matter of history, gave their sanction to the film, and it was decided to shoot some scenes and backgrounds in India, and then do matching material in Hollywood and in Lone Pine, California. Flynn and Paul Lukas went to India on location, but most of the other actors—

including thirteen-year-old Dean Stockwell, who played Kim—performed only in California.

The Rudyard Kipling tale is about a young orphan, Kim, the son of an Irish sergeant during the period of Victorian colonialism, who roams the bazaars and byways of India disguised as a native. He participates in intrigue involving an Afghan horse dealer who also functions as a secret agent

With Dean Stockwell

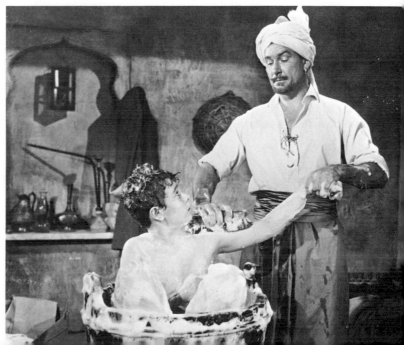

(Flynn), a holy lama on a quest (Lukas), and the British intelligence service in a counterplot against Czarist Russian encroachers who are stirring up trouble at the Khyber Pass.

The loose and ambiguous script seemed to ramble, and the direction merely underscored the generally unconvincing and leaden proceedings.

Flynn, though receiving top billing, had little to do in a distinctly supporting role. He did, however, have opportunity to sport a red beard, close-cropped and dyed gray hair, turbans, and colorful Indian garments.

The integrating of India, Lone Pine, and MGM was the most interesting aspect of the production.

With Dean Stockwell and Paul Lukas

With Robert Douglas, Reginald Owen, and Dean Stockwell

With Dean Stockwell and Ivan Triesault

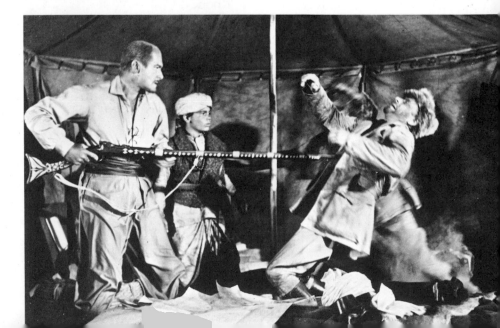

172

Hello God

1951 Written, Produced, Directed, and Narrated by William Marshall. Directors of Photography: Paul Ivano and Henry Freulich (U.S.) and Leo Barboni (Italy). Sound: Victor Appel. Running time: 64 minutes.

CAST *The Man on Anzio Beach*
ERROL FLYNN
The Little Italian Girl   Sherry Jackson
with Joe Muzzuca, Armando Formica

THIS curious film has never been released in the United States due to legal hassles, although it had been shown in Europe on occasion.

When Flynn finished work on *Kim*'s Indian location shots in early 1950, he came back to Hollywood for the remainder of the shooting by way of Italy, where he stopped off to appear in a picture under a partnership deal with ex-actor turned producer-writer-director, William Marshall. Marshall had made an early screen appearance in Flynn's *Santa Fe Trail*.

The resulting sixty-four minute semidocumentary plea for pacifism concerns an "unknown soldier" (Flynn) who tells of the thoughts, hopes, and aspirations of four young soldiers who were shot down in their attempt to reach Anzio Beach during World War II. As they approach heaven, the soldiers ask to be accepted, though they have arrived long before they were permitted to complete their lives on earth.

Apparently Flynn wanted to break his Warner contract at the time (which stipulated that his outside films must be first-class, major studio productions), but later, after negotiating a revised agreement, Flynn decided that the release of *Hello God* would be detrimental to his career. While working on another film with Marshall in France *(Captain Fabian)*, he allegedly arranged to have the negative of *Hello God* picked up at the laboratory in Hollywood by a friend, Charles Gross. Marshall retaliated by suing and by reconstructing the film, using out-takes and additional material shot in Santa Barbara and Hollywood. Flynn filed a cross-complaint to block the release, stating that Marshall had fraudulently represented details regarding the production. He also claimed that he did not realize that the subject of the film would be detrimental to the public welfare, in that it was of a pacifist nature and contrary to the foreign policy of the United States. Finally, he contended that the film was of poor quality and couldn't be improved.

The suits were never completely settled, and *Hello God* drifted into obscurity.

Adventures of Captain Fabian

With Micheline Presle

1951 A Silver Films Production. Released by Republic Pictures. Produced and Directed by William Marshall. Associate Producer: Robert Dorfmann. Screenplay by Errol Flynn. Based on the novel *Fabulous Ann Madlock* by Robert Shannon. Music by René Cloerec. Director of Photography: Marcel Grignon. Film Editor: Henri Taverna. Sets: Eugene Lourie and Max Douy. Costumes: Arlington Valles. Sound: Roger Cosson. Technical Collaborator: Guy Seitz. Production Supervisor: R. E. Marshall. Assistant Director and Technical Adviser: Marc Maurette. Production Manager: Sacha Kamenka. Assistant Production Manager: Jean Rossi. Running time: 100 minutes.

CAST

Captain Michael Fabian	ERROL FLYNN
Lea Marriotte	MICHELINE PRESLE
George Brissac	Vincent PRICE
Aunt Jesebel	Agnes MOOREHEAD
Henri Brissac	Victor FRANCEN
Constable Gilpin	Jim Gerald
Madam Pirott	Helena Manson
Emil	Howard Vernon
Phillipe	Roger Blin
Housekeeper	Valentine Camax
Judge Jean Brissac	Georges Flateau
Cynthia Winthrop	Zanie Campan
Constant	Reggie Nalder
Defense Attorney	Charles Fawcett
Mate	Aubrey Bower

With Agnes Moorehead

THE second film made in partnership with William Marshall, *Captain Fabian,* is undoubtedly one of the dullest pictures extant.

Flynn is credited with the adaptation and screenplay, although a friend and previous associate, Charles Gross, filed suit in November, 1951, claiming back payments due for working on the adaptation of the novel upon which the film was based.

Why Flynn would want credit, justified or not, on such an old-fashioned, stilted piece of claptrap is something to ponder. The story, to be as brief as possible, tells of a sea captain (Flynn) whose father had been defrauded by a wealthy New Orleans family. The captain returns to New Orleans, saves a servant girl from a murder charge, and then becomes embroiled in her course of revenge, which coincidentally has the same object as his: the wealthy New Orleans family.

Flynn plays with little spirit or conviction, and there is virtually no action until the last reel.

The exteriors representing New Orleans were re-created in the French city of Villefranche. For the interiors the company moved to the Victorine Studio in Nice and the Billancourt Studio in Paris.

After considerable difficulties, Marshall secured permission from the French government to make a single version in English rather than the customary French and English editions. Originally, Robert Florey was to direct the two versions, and actually started the English production, but not long afterward producer Marshall took over the directorial reins.

With Micheline Presle

Mara Maru

With Ruth Roman

1952   A Warner Brothers-First National Picture. Directed by Gordon Douglas. Produced by David Weisbart. Screenplay by N. Richard Nash. Based on an original story by Philip Yordan, Sidney Harmon, and Hollister Noble. Music by Max Steiner. Director of Photography: Robert Burks. Film Editor: Robert Swanson. Art Direc-tor: Stanley Fleischer. Set Decorator: Lyle B. Reifsnider. Miss Roman's Wardrobe: Milo Anderson. Make-up: Gordon Bau. Sound: C. A. Riggs. Special Effects: H. F. Koenekamp. Orchestrations: Murray Cutter. Assistant Director: William Kissel. Running time: 98 minutes.

With Robert Cabal and Henry Marco

With Paul Picerni, Raymond Burr, and Nestor Paiva

CAST	
Gregory Mason	ERROL FLYNN
Stella Callahan	RUTH ROMAN
Brock Benedict	Raymond Burr
Steven Ranier	Paul Picerni
Andy Callahan	Richard Webb
Lieutenant Zuenon	Dan Seymour
Ortega	Georges Renavent
Manuelo	Robert Cabal
Perol	Henry Marco
Captain Van Hoten	Nestor Paiva
Fortuno	Howard Chuman
Big China	Michael Ross

FLYNN played a deep-sea diver engaged in Philippine salvage operations after World War II. He alone knows exactly where a PT boat, laden with an extraordinary cross of diamonds, was sunk in the China Sea. A rich but dishonorable character (Burr) talks Flynn into piloting a craft to the scene of the loot. From that point on it becomes not only a question of finding the treasure, but of surviving the voyage with its many natural and imposed hazards and clashes of greed.

The film ends with Flynn, in a last-minute act of redemption, returning the cross to its rightful place in the church, and then walking off with his dead partner's wife (Roman).

The story had promise, but the script development contained reels of dull talk. Director Gordon Douglas adroitly took advantage of every opportunity to milk what action and underwater sequences there were.

In the last third of the picture Flynn does some solid acting as a man driven by greed, but it was apparent that Warners had little regard for Flynn or his vehicles at this stage of the game.

The location work was done at Los Angeles and Newport Harbors, Catalina Island and San Fernando Mission (doubling for a Manila cathedral).

With Maureen O'Hara

Against All Flags

1952   A Universal-International Picture. Technicolor. Directed by George Sherman. Produced by Howard Christie. Screenplay by Aeneas MacKenzie and Joseph Hoffman. Based on an original story by Aeneas MacKenzie. Music by Hans J. Salter. Director of Photography: Russell Metty. Special Photography: David S. Horsley. Dialogue Director: Irwin Berwick. Film Editor: Frank Gross. Art Directors: Bernard Herzbrun and Alexander Golitzen. Set Decorators: Russell A. Gausman and Oliver Emert. Costumes: Edward Stevenson. Make-up: Bud Westmore. Hair Styles: Joan St. Oegger. Sound: Leslie I. Carey and Joe Lapis. Assistant Directors: John Sherwood, Phil Bowles, and James Welch. Color Consultant: William Fritzsche. Unit Production Manager: Percy Ikerd. Running time: 83 minutes.

With Anthony Quinn

With Maureen O'Hara

CAST				
Brian Hawke	ERROL FLYNN	*Sir Cloudsley*	Lester Matthews
Spitfire Stevens	MAUREEN O'HARA	*William*	Tudor Owen
Roc Brasiliano	Anthony QUINN	*Captain Moisson*	Maurice Marsac
Princess Patma	Alice Kelley	*Captain Hornsby*	James Craven
Molvina MacGregor	Mildred Natwick	*Barber*	James Fairfax
Captain Kidd	Robert Warwick	*Swaine*	Michael Ross
Gow	Harry Cording	*Hassan*	Bill Radovich
Harris	John Alderson	*Crop-Ear Collins*	Paul Newlan
Jones	Phil Tully		

FOLLOWING James Stewart's precedent-setting deal in 1950 at Universal, Flynn accepted a similar percentage of the profits arrangement, in addition to a salary, at the same studio for this film.

Flynn played an eighteenth-century British naval officer, disguised as a deserter, who infiltrates a Madagascar stronghold of notorious pirates led by Quinn and O'Hara. He joins the buccaneers in a raid on the ship of the emperor of India, conceals the identity of the emperor's daughter (Kelley), and later sabotages the pirate cannons guarding the Madagascar harbor. Saving the princess, he then signals the British invasion, sails off with Maureen, and leaves the trade route clear for the British merchant fleet.

Near the conclusion, a double for Flynn does a less than effective reprise of an old Douglas Fairbanks stunt performed in *The Black Pirate* (1926). The hero, up on a yardarm, plunges his rapier into the sail of the ship and, clinging to the hilt, rides the rapier in a descent as it slits the sail from top to bottom.

All of the ingredients were directed and photographed in an undistinguished manner on the Universal stages and back lot and at Palos Verdes on the sea coast.

According to producer Howard Christie, Flynn was cooperative, prepared, and interested during the production. He broke his left ankle while performing in an action sequence on the deck of the pirate ship only five days prior to the end of shooting; and while he was out, the ship on the back lot used in the film was altered, and another pirate story was concocted and filmed with essentially the same crew *(Yankee Buccaneer)*. Later, the ship was changed to look as it did originally, and the final shooting on *Against All Flags,* with a healed Flynn, was resumed five months after the accident.

Against All Flags was remade in 1967 as *King's Pirate* with Doug McClure in Flynn's role and stock footage from the original inserted on occasion.

Cruise of the Zaca

1952　A Warner Brothers Picture. Print by Technicolor. Directed and Narrated by Errol Flynn. Supervised by Gordon Hollingshead. Written by Owen Crump. Music by Howard Jackson. Film Editor: Rex Steele. Sound: Charles David Forrest. Runnng time: 20 minutes.

IN the spring of 1946 Flynn decided to make a 16mm feature in color detailing a cruise down the coast of Mexico to the South Seas on his recently purchased 118-foot auxiliary schooner, *Zaca*.

Flynn's father, Professor Theodore Thomson Flynn, then dean of the faculty of science at Queen's University in Belfast, Ireland, was invited to participate during his vacation in this combination adventure and scientific expedition.

The California Scripps Institute of Oceanography provided equipment to make detailed studies of equatorial marine life, and Flynn started gathering an unusual assortment of people to set sail in August, 1946.

In addition to Flynn, his wife Nora, and his father, the roster included John Decker, Flynn's carousing artist friend, Howard Hill, the archer, Professor Carl L. Hubbs of the Scripps Institute, Charles Gross, a friend of Flynn's named director of the proposed film, and Jerry Corneya, a 16mm cameraman.

After a month of sailing, many of the group,

divorce in 1948, did not release it until December, 1952, over six years after it was started. Flynn, in the meantime, had married his third wife, Pat, but Nora was still in some of the telescoped footage.

The final version, running only twenty minutes and blown up to 35mm Technicolor, starts with Flynn taking off from his Mulholland grounds in a Paul Mantz helicopter bound for the Scripps Institute in La Jolla. While shooting some still pictures from the helicopter of whales off the coast, Flynn falls into the ocean and is promptly rescued. The group then sets sail on the *Zaca,* the first stop being San Benito Island, where elephant seal are found. Then various sea specimens are shown en route to the Panama Canal. The second half deals entirely with Port Antonio, Jamaica. Flynn and Nora take a small boat trip, hike by a picturesque waterfall, and witness the natives performing a traditional dance.

Certain aspects of *Cruise of the Zaca* recall *Vagabonding on the Pacific with John Barrymore,* a 1926 two-reel silent short, supposedly shot, edited, and titled by Barrymore, and dealing with a yachting trip he made to Mexico.

including Flynn's wife and father, returned home, but the actor continued his odyssey, changed his course, went through the Panama Canal and headed for Cap-Haitien. The edge of a hurricane tossed the craft off Jamaica. Flynn was entranced with the island in the East Indies, and finished his film there during an on-and-off lapse of time.

Before heading for the Panama Canal, Flynn had an extended layover in Acapulco, where Columbia Pictures had contracted for the *Zaca* to be used for many scenes in Orson Welles's *The Lady from Shanghai,* starring Rita Hayworth (Mrs. Welles at the time).

Warners bought the 16mm Kodachrome film of *Cruise of the Zaca,* but, due to Nora's filing for

With Professor Carl Hubbs and Flynn's father— Professor Theodore Thomson Flynn

Deep Sea Fishing

With Howard Hill

Supervision: Howard Hill. Narration: Bob Edge. Running time: 10 minutes.

FILMED in 16mm Kodachrome near Acapulco during Flynn's lengthy *Cruise of the Zaca* project, this curious ten-minute short shows archer Howard Hill and Flynn leaving the *Zaca* and boarding a small launch to fish for marlin and sail fish. Hill demonstrates his bow and arrow method of going after marine life (including slow motion studies), while Flynn, not having much success with that particular style, sticks with rod and reel.

Because his Warner contract prohibited appearances of this sort, Flynn's name is never mentioned by the commentator in this inconsequential, amateurishly produced and narrated item.

Flynn's close association with champion archer Howard Hill went back to the making of *Robin Hood*. Hill taught Flynn how to use a bow, and over the years the two hunted wild boar on Catalina Island, mountain lions in the Rockies, shark in the Pacific, barracuda in the Atlantic. They even went after fish underwater with their weapons.

*Flynn with his mother and father. In the center of the
picture are Joanne Dru and a visitor. Taken in England
on the set of* The Warriors *in late 1954.*

Part Four

The Last Seven Years

Flynn in August, 1957, just prior to suing Confidential *magazine for libel.*

WHENEVER he was asked why he had become an actor Errol Flynn would seem a little uncomfortable. Most of the time he deftly avoided answering personal questions and warded them off with quips. But to this question he once replied, "I don't know. I suppose most of us act all our lives. We have a façade, a front. We imagine ourselves to be what we're not, don't we?"

Flynn was enigmatic and contradictory. After he had died, Alexis Smith, his leading lady in three films, remembered a remark of his that indicated his fatalistic attitude toward life. He had had a mild heart attack during the making of *Gentleman Jim*. "Everybody was more concerned about it than he was. I said to him, 'You'll have to take care of yourself. Don't you want to live to be an old man?' He said, 'No, I like this half of life best and I want to live it to the hilt.'"

Patric Knowles, who began his Hollywood career playing Flynn's brother in *The Charge of the Light Brigade*, remembers Flynn as a man who lived life as if it were a game. "It was a game he enjoyed playing. But he was an impatient player—not to win, but to move on to the next bout."

If Flynn had played the part of *Don Juan* well, it was possibly because he understood the character of the part, knowing, perhaps like Don Juan himself, that the reputation of Great Lover is something of a joke and a bit of a bore. He joked about his wives and girl friends but he once confessed that although he was hopelessly and helplessly polygamous, he genuinely admired those who were happily monogamous. He also surprised people with his views about drinking: he felt alcohol should not be so readily available and he spoke in favor of prohibition.

Although Flynn was often heard to say he had no regrets about the way he had lived his life, his periodic despondency and his perpetual drinking suggested otherwise. He had reason in his own eyes to consider himself something of a failure. He had failed to be taken seriously as an actor, he had failed to win much attention with his writing, and he had failed badly as a husband. The good luck of his early years seemed to gradually slip away from him.

Failure hit Flynn with stunning impact in 1953 with the collapse of his own production of *William Tell*. He had sunk his cash assets in this large-scale historical epic and lost them all. It was also at this time that the United States government brought charges against him, claiming $840,000 in back taxes. Flynn disposed of some of his properties and gradually worked off his debts. Among the assets he liquidated was the house in the Hollywood Hills.

The basic Flynn home from the end of 1952 to the end of 1956 was the *Zaca*. For long stretches of that time he cruised the Mediterranean, drink-

Flynn in Rome in December, 1954, with Patrice Wymore and their one-year-old daughter, Arnella.

ing continuously and drifting spiritually. Every now and then he would proceed to some location to make a film, but in general it was a four-year period that Flynn considered the least inspired chapter of his life.

Errol Flynn needed luck at this point in his despondency. He doubted he would get it. He was, however, on the verge of an upward trend. After months of doing almost nothing, he one day received an offer to star in a film to be called *Istanbul*. He accepted, thinking the film would be made in Turkey, and that he would therefore sail the *Zaca* from Majorca to Istanbul. Flynn was forever interested in travel and he couldn't resist the temptation to visit somewhere in the world he had never before seen. But he found this Istanbul was a city mostly located on the back lot of Universal in Hollywood. It seemed to him that he had been tricked into returning to the place he had previously renounced.

Istanbul was a mediocre film but it put Flynn back into circulation and he found he was not, as he had supposed, unwanted and washed up. Perhaps thinking that the time was right to move into television he proceeded with a series, *The Errol Flynn Theatre*. He introduced each thirty-minute episode and acted in six of them. Cheaply produced in England, the one-season series was syndicated but never given prime network time.

Flynn probably considered it another of his follies.

The film that brought Flynn his first rave notices in years was *The Sun Also Rises*. It also resulted in the phenomenon known in the entertainment business as a "comeback"—the emotion-charged resurgence in popularity of a formerly big star. Darryl F. Zanuck made the decision to hire Flynn against the advice of many who considered him a bad risk and unable to give a deep, sustained characterization. Patrice Wymore says, "He was terrified of accepting the role, and I had to talk him into it and give him a bit of encouragement."

Flynn married Patrice Wymore in Monte Carlo in October, 1950. Although he had protested loudly and eloquently his resistance to marriage, he knew he needed the dignity of a well-adjusted relationship with a suitable wife. He would later admit that this third failure at marriage was no fault of actress-singer Wymore, and he would compliment her for staying with him through the most unsettled period of his life. She would discover, as did few people, what Flynn was really like behind his cloak of seeming confidence. "I found generally that when he was at his lowest ebb or most frightened he would appear to be at his gayest. I had to know him quite some time before I was able to recognize his low ebbs."

As Flynn's career picked up, his marriage to

Patrice Wymore ran down. He seemed to lose interest in his wife and their daughter, Arnella, and drifted away from them, but he announced no formal separation. Wymore spoke for everyone who had known and suffered from Flynn's cavalier manner when she said, "I wish I could hate him but I can't." She continued, "He could charm the birds out of the trees. But he was an adventurer with people. There was a perpetual imp about him, and he loved to tease. Looking back on it, I don't think he should ever have got married. He was simply too mercurial. He liked to be by himself or with his old cronies to chew the fat, or whatever men do when they are together. I felt out of it completely."

With *The Sun Also Rises,* the Flynn tide had turned. Next came *Too Much, Too Soon,* which took him back to Warners, and it was while making this picture that he met the girl who would become his companion for the remaining two years of his life—Beverly Aadland. Working as a bit player in *Marjorie Morningstar,* Beverly was fifteen but she had a maturity of appearance and personality beyond her years. The child of a broken home and with several years behind her as an entertainer, she was then, as now, a bright and feisty girl. Asked what he, a man of his age and background, saw in a girl of fifteen, Flynn merely said, "She amuses me." Her own lively nature acted as a lift to a man who was aging rapidly.

Early in 1958 Flynn agreed to star in the stage play *The Master of Thornfield,* which his millionaire friend Huntington Hartford had adapted from *Jane Eyre.* The play tried out in Detroit and Cincinnati, but Flynn left it before it got to New York. He claimed that it was a poor vehicle, with which opinion no critic disagreed, but it was also true that Flynn by this time was incapable of memorizing a lengthy text and his performance was an embarrassment.

Darryl F. Zanuck came to Flynn's rescue with an offer to star him in *The Roots of Heaven,* which Flynn gladly accepted because it gave him a reason to leave the Hartford play. After several months in Africa and Europe making *The Roots of Heaven,* Flynn went to Cuba to work on what would be his last, and sorriest, film, *Cuban Rebel Girls.*

Since Flynn was both a frustrated writer and a man who had lead a colorful and highly publicized life, it was inevitable that he would leave an

Flynn with Beverly Aadland at her seventeenth birthday party in September, 1959.

autobiography and just as inevitable that it would have an assured and eager market. But the concentration needed to write such a volume was now beyond Flynn. Late in 1958 the New York publishing house of Putnam, which had given Flynn an advance on a product that didn't seem to be forthcoming, approached Earl Conrad with the offer of collaborating on the book. Conrad, a veteran journalist and author, had made most of his reputation with his book *Scottsboro Boy,* written with and about Haywood Patterson, the Alabama Negro who was the central figure in the infamous Scottsboro case. Putnam obviously felt that such a writer was needed for the complex Flynn saga. Conrad accepted the offer and proceeded to spend ten weeks with Flynn at his estate near Port Antonio, Jamaica.

Errol Flynn had always been a puzzle to those who knew him, and he seldom revealed his inner nature to anyone. Working with Conrad on what emerged as a surprisingly candid autobiography, it was now necessary for Flynn to open up. What Conrad saw was a man with a collection of disparate personalities, a man who could in a short space of time be hilarious and despondent, a man who could be very kind and very cruel—especially to women. He was a vulgarian at one hour of the day and a cultured gentleman at another, a rough fun-lover who was also amazingly knowledgeable. "He was one of the most poetic men I have ever met, and he could describe trees and flowers and the wonders of the ocean in the most beautiful language," says Conrad.

What had fame done to Errol Flynn? According to Conrad, it's possible that the life Flynn had lived was too much for any one man. "He had too much fortune, too much adulation, too much sensual indulgence, too much everything. Finally he was consumed by it all. Then he had the problem of living up to the reputation he had come by as an international fun figure, as a colorful personality who should provide headlines for the public every few weeks or months. This produced in him a great tension and strain. It all helped to give him an image he didn't really want, and in time he became a ripped-out-at-the-seams caricature of himself."

The trouble with Flynn, in Conrad's view, was the difference between the inner man and the public image. There was desolation beneath the bravado. In particular, Flynn regretted the Casanova identification, and Conrad believes the affect of the rape trial set off a spiritual deterioration in the man. Flynn had often been described as the most beautiful man since Apollo, but it was a description that caused him to cringe. Conrad noticed that Flynn avoided looking in mirrors or at pictures of himself; he seemed to resent the looks that had made him famous, and unlike many actors he kept no scrapbooks. He told Conrad he would rather have written two or three good books than made all his sixty films. "Everyone in the world felt they knew Flynn; his life was an open newspaper, yet he was really a lonely man—on top, but alone—and hardly anyone knew this about him. He would often wander off by himself, and in all the time I was with him he seemed to get very little mail, except for bills and business notes."

Earl Conrad spent nine months putting *My Wicked, Wicked Ways* together from the more than 200,0000 words of notes that had been compiled and transcribed by two court stenographers whom Conrad had hired to sit in on the daily interviewing. With these notes Conrad was able to retain Flynn's own style of storytelling. In the summer of 1959 Flynn visited New York to confer with the publishers and check the galleys.

Flynn then proceeded to Hollywood to perform

In The Golden Shanty

his last work as an actor. This was a thirty-minute television picture, *The Golden Shanty,* in which he played a peddler and confidence man traveling the Wild West in a supply wagon.

The Golden Shanty was shot on a three-day schedule and the director, Arthur Hiller, recalls the filming as a disturbing experience. "Flynn was in such poor health I thought it unfair of his agent to send him out on a job like this. He couldn't remember his lines, and it was painful to watch this once graceful athlete barely able to climb out of a wagon." Despite the tribulations, Hiller was glad he had this one chance to work with Flynn. "Even then he had the charm of a mischievous small boy, humorous and impossible to dislike." One incident in the making of this film is remembered by Hiller as particularly sad. "We had a barroom sequence and Flynn and the leading lady were supposed to converse as they danced back and forth and around the bar. I set up teleprompters at various points so that Errol could read his lines no matter which way he was facing. He was hopelessly confused. After several minutes of this he put his head down on the bar, and when a few moments later he looked up at me he had tears in his eyes, and he said, 'Arthur, I can't do it, I can't do it. I just don't know what I'm doing.' "

190

Flynn made one more professional appearance. In the first week of October, 1959, he was a guest on Red Skelton's television show, playing a gentleman tramp in a comedy sketch about life in a hobo camp. The following week he and Beverly went to Vancouver, B.C., to meet a Canadian businessman who was interested in buying the *Zaca* for $100,000. Although he claimed he needed the money to make a divorce settlement with his wife, Flynn probably wanted to be free of the cost and trouble of maintaining the boat. The agreement to purchase the *Zaca* was at this stage verbal; no papers had been signed. The yacht was still moored at Majorca—and would remain there for years to come.

On the afternoon of October 14, while being driven to the Vancouver airport, Flynn complained of severe pains in his back and asked to be taken immediately to a doctor. He was taken to the home of Dr. Grant A. Gould, a friend of the man who wanted to buy the *Zaca*. Dr. Gould administered a pain-killing drug to Flynn. Then, feeling better but still stiff, Flynn stood in a doorway with his back resting against the jamb. In a good mood, he told a string of anecdotes about some of his favorite personalities, among them W. C. Fields and John Barrymore. After a while he told Dr. Gould he needed to lie down. The doctor took him to his bedroom and because of the sore back advised him to lie on the floor. Flynn then fell asleep, and it was a sleep from which he never awakened.

Death was attributed to a heart attack, but the autopsy revealed many contributing factors. Flynn had injured his back in a fall several years previously; he had suffered attacks of malaria plus occasional bouts with tuberculosis and gonorrhea. In his last years he had acute hepatitis, and there was little left of his liver and kidneys. The coroner expressed amazement that Flynn had been able to reach the age of fifty. He seemed to have thumbed his nose at medical science with his chain smoking, his use of narcotics, and his inordinate drinking. His constitution, like many other things about him, was extraordinary. He had lived as he pleased, and when the end came it, too, was the way he wanted—quick.

Errol Flynn was buried at Forest Lawn Cemetery on October 20, 1959, following a short and quiet service of Episcopal rites. Jack L. Warner delivered the eulogy and Dennis Morgan sang

Flynn at the airport in Vancouver, B. C., a few days before his death.

"Home is the Sailor." The pallbearers were Jack Oakie, Mickey Rooney, Flynn's attorney Justin Golenbock, director Raoul Walsh, Guinn (Big Boy) Williams, and restaurateur Mike Romanoff. Unlike the funerals of many Hollywood celebrities, Flynn's was noticeably restrained.

Shortly before he left to go to Vancouver, Flynn asked Nora Eddington to meet him. He wanted to tell her and their two daughters that his doctors in New York had advised him he had only a year left to live. Recalls Nora: "I hadn't seen him in about a year and he looked like an old, old man, absolutely terrible, and I didn't think he could last six months. But he was strutting like a cock and trying to be debonair. He knew he was dying but he wasn't going to scream and yell about it. I started to cry and he said, 'Don't be unhappy; you know I've lived twice and I've had a marvelous life.'"

191

The Master of Ballantrae

1953 A Warner Brothers Picture. Technicolor. Directed by William Keighley. Screenplay by Herb Meadow. Additional dialogue by Harold Medford. Based on the novel by Robert Louis Stevenson. Music by William Alwyn; conducted by Muir Mathieson. Director of Photography: Jack Cardiff. Film Editor: Jack Harris. Art Director: Ralph Brinton. Costumes: Margaret Furse. Make-up: George Frost. Sound:

Harold King. Assistant Director: Frank Mattison. Fencing Master: Patrick Crean. Color Consultant: Joan Bridge. Running time: 89 minutes.

CAST
Jamie Durrisdeer	ERROL FLYNN
Colonel Francis Burke	
	ROGER LIVESEY
Henry Durrisdeer	ANTHONY STEEL
Lady Alison	Beatrice CAMPBELL
Jessie Brown	Yvonne FURNEAUX
Lord Durrisdeer	Felix Aylmer
MacKellar	Mervyn Johns
Mendoza	Charles Goldner
Major Clarendon	Ralph Truman
Bull	Francis de Wolff
Arnaud	Jack Berthier
Marianne	Gillian Lynne
MacCauley	Moultrie Kelsall

AFTER finishing *Against All Flags* in mid-1952, Flynn took off for a protracted stay in Europe for a variety of reasons: to take advantage of U.S. income tax exemption, to avoid back-alimony suits and taxes, and to try his luck with

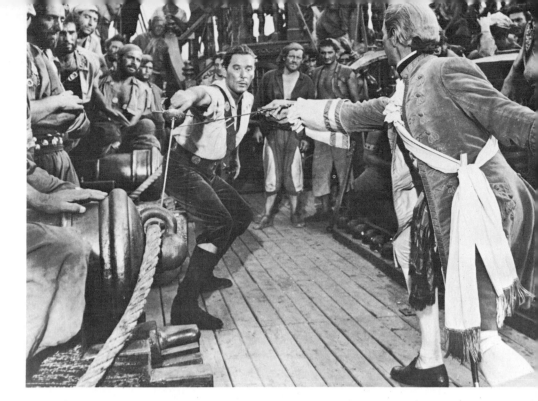

European production. His pictures had always fared well on the continent.

The Master of Ballantrae, produced in England to utilize frozen Warner funds, was Flynn's best all-round film since *Don Juan*. He played the master of Ballantrae Castle, described in Robert Louis Stevenson's novel as that "wicked, wicked lad," in a rather grim, determined, and underplayed manner.

constantly captivated the eye and compensated for some of the script's bleakness. The action sequences were profuse and reasonably well staged.

The exterior locations ranged from the Scottish Highlands at Dornie, Ballachulich, and Glen Coe, to Newquay in Cornwall and, for the pirate episodes, Palermo in Sicily. The interiors were shot in England.

Most critics were kind to Flynn and the film, but it did only fairly well at the box office in America. This was the last vehicle made under his Warner contract.

The master goes off to fight for the Stuarts in the British insurrection of 1745, while his young brother (Steel) remains loyal to King George II. By the time the master returns and is reunited with his brother, he has been given up for dead, escaped from the British in a smuggler's vessel, joined up with a band of buccaneers, looted a pirate galleon loaded with treasure, and escaped the hangman's noose.

Stevenson's novel is a somber tragedy of the enmity of two brothers. It ends with both of them dead after many incidents in various parts of the world. The script eliminates most of the labyrinthian ways of the novel, whitewashes the character of the brother portrayed by Flynn and softens the ending to allow both brothers to live.

Although Flynn did not swashbuckle with the élan of his younger days, the imaginative and picturesque Technicolor photography of Jack Cardiff

With Beatrice Campbell, Anthony Steel, and Felix Aylmer

With Roger Livesey and Ralph Truman

Crossed Swords

1954 A Viva Films Production. Released by United Artists. Pathécolor. Directed by Milton Krims. Produced by J. Barrett (Barry) Mahon and Vittorio Vassarotti. Associate Producers: Nato de Angelis and Arthur Villiesid. Original Screenplay by Milton Krims. Director of Photography: Jack Cardiff. Art Director: Arrigo Equini. Costumes: Nino Novarese. Make-up: C. Gambarelli. Hair Styles: Palumbi. Running time: 86 minutes.

CAST

Renzo	ERROL FLYNN	*Buio*	Silvio Bagolini
Francesca	GINA LOLLOBRIGIDA	*Spiga*	Renata Chiantioni
Raniero	Cesare Danova	*Miele*	Mimo Billi
Fulvia	Nadia Gray	*The Duke*	Pietro Tordi
Tomasina	Paola Mori	*Lenzi*	Ricardo Rioli
Pavoncello	Roldano Lupi		
Gennarelli	Alberto Rabagliati		

With Gina Lollobrigida

195

AFTER completing *The Master of Ballantrae* for Warners, Flynn teamed up with J. Barrett (Barry) Mahon to enter into co-production with some Italians on *Crossed Swords,* or, as it was originally titled in Europe, *Il Maestro di Don Giovanni.*

Since *Adventures of Don Juan* was so popular in European countries, the new swashbuckler was an attempt to recapture the spirit of its predecessor. Complete with some tongue-in-cheek balcony wooings, irate husbands, an evil counselor planning treason in an Italian dukedom, recurring swordplay, and a final put-down of the planned treason by Flynn, the attempt was largely unsuccessful due to a dull, strained script and unsure direction.

Nor was Flynn up to his chores any more as a dashing Don Juan. His romantic scenes with Gina Lollobrigida (the duke's daughter) lacked credibility.

The best feature of the production was Jack Cardiff's color photography, particularly the exteriors, which were filmed in the village of Lauro in the southern Italian hills.

Flynn later claimed that *Crossed Swords*'s lack of acceptance in America was due to the fact that it wasn't handled or sold properly.

William Tell

(Not Completed)

Director and Supervisor of Photography:
Jack Cardiff.

CAST *William Tell*　　ERROL FLYNN
Antonella Lualdi
Bruce Cabot
Aldo Fabrizi
Massimo Serato
Franco Interlenghi
Alberto Rabagliati
Vira Silenti
Dave Crowly

A PRODUCTION of *William Tell* was planned as the second of three films to be made in Europe by Flynn and his colleague Barry Mahon in conjunction with Italian producers for United Artists release.

Flynn supposedly wrote the outline for the script. It dealt with the legendary Swiss hero who, after having been forced to shoot an apple off his son's head, precipitated the general revolt which eventually won the Swiss their national independence in the 1300s. Schiller's play was obviously the basis for the outline.

Flynn also put up approximately $430,000 of his own money towards the budgeted $860,000 production in which he would play the title role.

His Italian partners were to provide the other $430,000.

Impressed with Jack Cardiff's arresting color photography on Flynn's recently completed *Master of Ballantrae* and *Crossed Swords* (to say nothing of his earlier work on *Black Narcissus* and *The Red Shoes*), the swashbuckler offered Cardiff the opportunity to direct his first film as well as serve as cameraman.

Flynn apparently was interested in making a quality film. He even decided to use CinemaScope before the initial feature made in that process—*The Robe*—was released.

Shooting started on exteriors in Northern Italy in June of 1953. After several weeks of filming, Flynn was politely informed by his Italian partners that the money had run out. According to Flynn, the actor discovered that the principal Italian investor had put up only $50,000 instead of his agreed-to share of $250,000, and he now wanted Flynn to put up the remainder. But the Italian backer still insisted on a full half of the final earnings, and he advised that he would sue any new investor!

Jack Cardiff states that after the money ran out he "carried on for about six more weeks—the crew working for nothing—until poverty forced us to quit the beautiful mountain location of Courmayeur, right beside Mont Blanc. I was two years waiting for the picture to start again while law suits—including my own—were bandied back and forth. But it all fizzled out. The Italian producer who let us down died bankrupt. I finally abandoned ship, being owed nine million lira."

Following the shutdown, Flynn tried to get additional financing for *William Tell*, but ran into problems and legal complications. Columbia's Harry Cohn, British producer-director Herbert Wilcox and representatives from United Artists came to Rome to look into the prospects, but all backed away upon hearing the demands of the Italians.

Somewhere, approximately thirty minutes of the edited Pathé color, CinemaScope feature rests, never completed, never publicly shown. One can only speculate on the potential.

With Anna Neagle

Let's Make Up

(Lilacs in the Spring)

1955   An Everest Pictures Production. Released by United Artists. (Released in Great Britain by Republic as *Lilacs in the Spring*.) Eastman Color. Produced and Directed by Herbert Wilcox. Screenplay by Harold Purcell. Based on the play *The Glorious Days* by Robert Nesbitt. Original music by Harry Parr Davies. Incidental score composed and arranged by Robert Farnon. Production numbers orchestrated and conducted by Harry Acres. Production numbers and dances devised and arranged by Philip and Betty Buchel. Director of Photography: Max Greene. Film Editor: Reginald Beck. Art Director: William C. Andrews. Assistant Art Directors: Leonard Townsend, Albert Witherick, and A. Van Montagu. Miss Neagle's Dresses: Anthony Holland. Wardrobe Supervisor: Maude Churchill. Make-up: Harold Fletcher. Hairdressing: Nora Bentley. Sound: Peter Handford and Len Shilton. Production Manager: J. D. Wilcox. Assistant Director: Frank Hol-lands. Unit Manager: Patricia Smith. Continuity: Phyllis Crocker. Running time: 94 minutes.

CAST		
Carole Beaumont		
Lillian Grey		ANNA NEAGLE
Queen Victoria		
Nell Gwyn		
John Beaumont		ERROL FLYNN
Charles King		DAVID FARRAR
King Charles		
Kate		Kathleen Harrison
Albert Gutman		Peter Graves
Prince Albert		
Lady Drayton		Helen Haye
Old George		Scott Sanders
1st Woman in Dress Circle		Alma Taylor
2nd Woman in Dress Circle		Hetty King
Hollywood Director		Alan Gifford
Young Carole		Jennifer Mitchell
Very Young Carole		Gillian Harrison
Hollywood Reporter		George Margo

199

With Anna Neagle

SHORTLY after losing approximately $430,000 of his own money on the *William Tell* debacle, Flynn discovered that his business manager allegedly had bilked him through the years, and he owed over $1 million in back income taxes and various other debts—including alimony payments to Lili Damita.

Determined not to declare bankruptcy, but no longer in demand for pictures, he was somewhat salvaged by an offer of England's perennial pro-ducer-director of musicalized sentimentality, Herbert Wilcox. Wilcox wanted Flynn to play opposite Anna Neagle (Wilcox's wife, and a great favorite with the British public) in an adaptation of her recent stage success, *The Glorious Days*. In exchange for the actor's services, Wilcox offered to help Flynn get partially disentangled from his monetary shambles, and even discussed financing the defunct *William Tell*.

Flynn gratefully responded, and during the

With Anna Neagle and David Farrar

200

With Anna Neagle

filming of *Lilacs in the Spring* he conducted himself in a relatively professional manner. The Wilcoxs and Errol and his third wife, Pat, became good friends.

For one sequence, Flynn was given an opportunity to sing and do a soft-shoe with Miss Neagle to "Lily of Laguna." He performed his musical chores—limited as they were—in an adequate fashion. Another number, a tango involving Flynn and Miss Neagle, was cut from the final released version.

Lilacs in the Spring emerged as a very old-fashioned backstage romance. The treatment is on a par with the material, reflecting a late Twenties or early Thirties sentimental musical. A somewhat confusing potpourri of flashbacks, bits of stage musicals, dance numbers, and just plain corn, it nevertheless contains a certain amount of nostalgic charm.

The film begins in black and white, with Miss Neagle as a World War II service performer who suffers a concussion during an air raid on London; and with a switch to color, she imagines herself to be Nell Gwyn (a role she had played in a 1935 Wilcox film). A short while later she has another blackout and imagines she is Queen Victoria (a role she played in two previous Wilcox films).

After recovering from this episode, she plays her own mother in the days when she was courted by and married to Flynn, who portrays a song-and-dance man of the provinces who elevates Neagle to stardom, but is forgotten by producers and public after his service in World War I. He leaves his wife when she refuses to go to Hollywood with him, and then he finds fame and fortune via the birth of the talkies. The film closes after the two lovers have a reconciliation.

In England, where Neagle received top billing, the picture did reasonably well; in America, where Flynn had top billing, and the title was changed to *Let's Make Up,* it was a flop with limited bookings.

The day after Flynn's death a few years later, producer-director Wilcox was quoted in a London newspaper as saying that "Errol Flynn was an outrageous personality." Wilcox went on to state that he would have been regarded as a fine actor "if his talent could have been disciplined. His love of living defeated his ability as an artist."

With Peter Finch and Joanne Dru

The Warriors

(The Dark Avenger)

1955   An Allied Artists Production. (Released in Great Britain by 20th Century-Fox as *The Dark Avenger.*) Eastman Color; Print by Technicolor; CinemaScope. Directed by Henry Levin. Produced by Walter Mirisch. Original Screenplay by Daniel B. Ullman. Music by Cedric Thorpe Davie; Conducted by Louis Levy. Director of Photography: Guy Green. Dialogue Coach: Esmond Knight. Film Editor: E. B. Jarvis. Art Director: Terence Verity. Set Decorator: Harry White. Costumes: Elizabeth Haffenden. Make-up: L. V. Clark. Hair Styles: Polly Young. Recording Supervisor: Harold King. Sound: Leslie Hammon and Len Shilton. Assistant Director: Terence Hunter. Technical Adviser: Charles R. Beard. Production Manager: Roy Parkinson. Continuity: Elaine Schreyeck. Second Unit Director: Alex Bryce. Second Unit Lighting Cameraman: Cyril J. Knowles. Lyric of Song "Bella Marie" by Christopher Hassall. Running time: 85 minutes.

With Joanne Dru

202

CAST
Prince Edward	ERROL FLYNN	*Libean*	Alastair Hunter
Lady Joan Holland	Joanne DRU	*Sir John*	Rupert Davies
Count de Ville	Peter FINCH	*D'Estell*	Ewan Solon
Marie	Yvonne Furneaux	*Thomas Holland*	Richard O'Sullivan
Sir Ellys	Patrick Holt	*Dubois*	Jack Lambert
King Edward III	Michael Hordern	*Gurd*	John Welsh
Sir Bruce	Moultrie Kelsall	*Arnaud*	Harold Kasket
Sir Philip	Robert Urquhart	*Francois Le Clerc*	Leslie Linder
John Holland	Vincent Winter	*First French Knight*	Robert Brown
Du Guesclin	Noel Willman	*Second French Knight*	John Phillips
Genevieve	Frances Rowe		

With Yvonne Furneaux

203

THE last of the Flynn swashbucklers, *The Warriors* has some assets. Filmed on colorful location sites in Hertfordshire, England, the production values and photography were quite lush.

Flynn, as Prince Edward of England (the so-called "Black Prince"), is left in France after the Hundred Years' War to guard the conquered lands of his father, Edward III. The French lords, led by the nonhistorical De Ville (Finch), spend all of the film trying to get rid of Prince Edward, who spends most of the film trying to rescue his lady-love (Dru) from De Ville's clutches.

The final siege on Edward's castle by De Ville and his cohorts was almost as good as a similar sequence depicting the storming of Torquilstone Castle in MGM's 1952 *Ivanhoe*. Indeed, the same castle built for *Ivanhoe* on the MGM Elstree lot, and left standing, was the setting for this sequence.

Unfortunately, *Ivanhoe* had spawned a number of imitators in the succeeding years, most of them vastly inferior; and by the time the reasonably well-done *Warriors* appeared, the cycle had been played out, and it received little attention.

Some critics remarked at the time that Flynn was getting too old for this kind of vehicle, an opinion shared by the actor.

King's Rhapsody

1955 An Everest Pictures Production. Released by United Artists. Eastman Color; CinemaScope. Produced and Directed by Herbert Wilcox. Screenplay by Pamela Bower and Christopher Hassall. Additional dialogue by A. P. Herbert. Based on the musical play by Ivor Novello. Songs by Ivor Novello and Christopher Hassall. Music arranged and conducted by Robert Farnon. Director of Photography: Max Greene. Film Editor: Reginald Beck. Art Director: William C. Andrews. Costumes: Anthony Holland. Choreography: Jon Gregory. Sound: Peter Handford, Len Shilton and Red Law. Running time: 93 minutes.

CAST
Marta Karillos	ANNA NEAGLE
King Richard	ERROL FLYNN
Princess Cristiane	PATRICE WYMORE
Queen Mother	Martita Hunt
King Paul	Finlay Currie
The Prime Minister	Francis de Wolff
Countess Astrid	Joan Benham
King Peter	Reginald Tate
Jules	Miles Malleson
Singer's voice	Edmund Hockridge

THE teaming of Flynn and Anna Neagle in *Lilacs in the Spring (Let's Make Up)*, although not successful in the United States, turned out to be fairly good box office in England. Producer-director Wilcox went ahead with plans to film their second vehicle while Flynn was shooting *The Warriors (The Dark Avenger)*.

King's Rhapsody, one of Ivor Novello's last musical plays, was even more old-fashioned than *Lilacs in the Spring* on the screen. A Ruritanian romance with all the creaking plot devices, it dealt with the somewhat alcoholic prince of "Laurentia" who accepts exile in order to live with the woman he loves (Neagle). After the death of his father, he returns to succeed to the throne and accept a

With Patrice Wymore

With Anna Neagle

With Patrice Wymore

marriage to a princess whom he doesn't at first care about (Wymore), but then grows to love. Years later, exiled in Paris, he meets his former mistress, who, in order to persuade him to return to his kingdom to see the coronation of his son, untruthfully tells him she is married. The king returns to his country and realizes he belongs with his wife and son. (In the play, he returns, but is purposely unrecognized, and remains alone in the cathedral after the coronation as the curtain falls.)

As was customary in early CinemaScope films, scenes between two or three people were played for several minutes in a master long shot with little movement of camera or people, and little or no intercutting of closeups.

Anna Neagle's musical numbers were deleted from the final released version, and she was left

with merely a supporting role. Flynn and Patrice Wymore (the third Mrs. Flynn) carried the bulk of the picture. Flynn was convincing in a few scenes, but he appeared dispirited in most.

This was Wymore's second and last appearance in a feature with her husband (the first was *Rocky Mountain),* although she did appear in several TV films with him. In *King's Rhapsody* she was beautifully coiffured and costumed and photographed quite lovely. Virtually all the numbers left in the final version were sung and danced by her.

Most of the exteriors were photographed in and near Barcelona in Spain. The interiors were done in England.

A major flop everywhere, *King's Rhapsody* seemed to vindicate the belief that Flynn was now completely washed up as a box-office attraction.

*With Finlay Currie
and Martita Hunt*

Istanbul

With Cornell Borchers

1956 A Universal-International Picture. Technicolor; CinemaScope. Directed by Joseph Pevney. Produced by Albert J. Cohen. Screenplay by Seton I. Miller, Barbara Gray, and Richard Alan Simmons. Based on a story by Seton I. Miller. Director of Photography: William Daniels. Special Photography: Clifford Stine. Dialogue Director: Leon Charles. Film Editor: Sherman Todd. Art Directors: Alexander Golitzen and Eric Orbom. Set Decorators: Russell A. Gausman and Julia Heron. Costumes: William Thomas. Make-up: Bud Westmore. Hair Styles: Joan St. Oegger. Music Supervision: Joseph Gershenson. Songs (sung by Nat King Cole): "I Was a Little Too Lonely," by Jay Livingston and Ray Evans; "When I Fall in Love," by Victor Young and Edward Heyman. Assistant Directors: Joseph E. Kenny and Ray de Camp. Color Consultant: William Fritzsche. Unit Production Manager: Lew Leary. Running time: 84 minutes.

With Cornell Borchers and Nat (King) Cole

With John Bentley and
Cornell Borchers

CAST *James Brennan*   ERROL FLYNN
    Stephanie Bauer

               CORNELL BORCHERS

Inspector Nural	John Bentley
Douglas Fielding	Torin Thatcher
Charlie Boyle	Leif Erickson
Marge Boyle	Peggy Knudsen
Mr. Darius	Martin Benson
Danny Rice	Nat King Cole
Paul Renkov	Werner Klemperer
Aziz Rakim	Vladimir Sokoloff
Kazim	Jan Arvan
Ali	Nico Minardos
Lieutenant Sarac	Ted Hecht
Dr. Sarica	David Bond
Mr. Florian	Roland Varno
Stewardess	Hillevi Rombin

UNIVERSAL dusted off the script of a 1947 Fred MacMurray and Ava Gardner melodrama, *Singapore,* changed the locale to Turkey, shot some background scenes there in color, and offered Flynn the opportunity to do his first film in Hollywood since *Against All Flags* in 1952, also for Universal.

The result was a second-rate melodrama, with merely an adequate and subdued performance by Flynn. He played an American pilot-adventurer who purchases an oriental bracelet in which he discovers thirteen valuable diamonds. (In *Singapore* it was pearls.) For his suspected participation in the intrigue conducted by both customs officers and smugglers to recover the stones, he is deported. Five years later he returns to retrieve the jewels hidden in his hotel room and once again becomes involved in plots and counterplots. Added complications center around his wife (Borchers), who is now a victim of amnesia, and who, in the intervening five years, has married another man (Thatcher).

With Werner Klemperer and
Martin Benson

The Big Boodle

1957 A Monteflor Production. Released by United Artists. Directed by Richard Wilson. Produced by Lewis F. Blumberg. Screenplay by Jo Eisinger. Based on the novel by Robert Sylvester. Music by Raul Lavista. Director of Photography: Lee Garmes. Film Editor: Charles L. Kimball. Sound: Manuel Topete Blake. Make-up: Anita Guerrero. Production Supervisor: Henry Spitz. Production Coordinator: Alberto Montes. Assistant Director: Henry Hartman. Script Supervisor: Bobby Sierks. Running time: 83 minutes.

CAST

Ned Sherwood	ERROL FLYNN
Colonel Mastegui	
	PEDRO ARMENDARIZ
Fina Ferrer	ROSSANA RORY
Anita Ferrer	GIA SCALA
Armando Ferrer	Sandro Giglio
Miguel Collada	Jacques Aubuchon
Carlos Rubi	Carlos Rivas
Griswold	Charles Todd
Casino Manager	
	Guillerme Alvarez Guedes
Chuchu	Carlos Mas
Salcito	Rogelio Hernandez
Secretary	Velia Martinez
Sales Girl	Aurora Pita

With Rossana Rory

With Pedro Armendariz (left)

THE BIG BOODLE's only distinction is that a good deal of it was filmed in Havana (before Castro became Premier), with a final chase and gun battle making prolonged use of the famed Morro Castle.

Flynn plays a croupier in a Havana gambling casino who is handed five hundred counterfeit pesos from a blonde player (Rory), and is then suspected of knowing where the bogus plates are located, as well as being in on an elaborate counterfeit plot. Flynn decides to pursue an inquiry into the mystery. From this point on the film is one long, mysterious chase, during the course of which the camera drinks in a tour of the streets and plazas of Havana, its night clubs, gambling dens, assorted traps, palaces, and monuments of historical interest.

Some American reviewers (particularly *Newsweek*'s) who evidently had not seen Flynn's European films of the preceding few years, commented on his "heaviness of face, jowliness and weariness of eye which gave him a new credibility."

With Gia Scala

The Sun Also Rises

1957   A 20th Century-Fox Picture. Cinema-Scope; Color by DeLuxe. Directed by Henry King. Produced by Darryl F. Zanuck. Screenplay by Peter Viertel. Based on the novel by Ernest Hemingway. Music by Hugo Friedhofer; Conducted by Lionel Newman; Orchestrated by Maurice de Packh. Spanish music by Alexander Courage; Orchestrated by Bernard Mayers and Arthur Morton. Guitar music by Vicente Gomez. Director of Photography: Leo Tover. Film Editor: William Mace. Art Directors: Lyle R. Wheeler and Mark-Lee Kirk. Set Decorators: Walter M. Scott, Paul S. Fox, and Jack Stubbs. Executive Wardrobe Designer: Charles

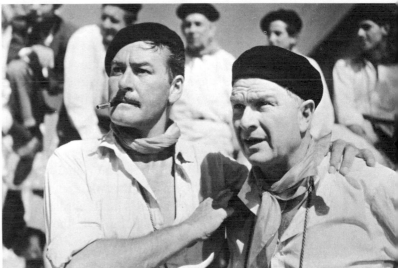

With Eddie Albert

With Tyrone Power

211

LeMaire. Ava Gardner's Wardrobe: Fontana Sisters, Rome. Make-up: Jack Obringer. Hair Styles: Gladys Rasmussen. Sound: Bernard Freericks and Frank Moran. Assistant Director: Stanley Hough. Bullfight sequences staged by Miguel Delgado. Brass bands directed by Ramon Hernandez. Color Consultant: Leonard Doss. Running time: 129 minutes.

CAST		
Jake Barnes	TYRONE POWER
Lady Brett Ashley	AVA GARDNER
Robert Cohn	MEL FERRER
Mike Campbell	ERROL FLYNN
Bill Gorton	EDDIE ALBERT
Count Mippipopolous	Gregory Ratoff
Georgette	Juliette Greco
Zizi	Marcel Dalio
Doctor	Henry Daniell
Harris	Bob Cunningham
The Girl	Danik Patisson
Pedro Romero	Robert Evans
Mr. Braddock	Eduardo Noriega
Mrs. Braddock	Jacqueline Evans
Montoya	Carlos Muzquiz
Frances	Rebecca Iturbi
Romero's Manager	Carlos David Ortigos

With Eddie Albert

FLYNN was at his professional (and perhaps personal) nadir when Darryl Zanuck, for whom he had never worked and hardly knew, asked him to play Mike Campbell, the boozy, happy-go-lucky bankrupt in *The Sun Also Rises*. He even accepted, after a struggle, fourth billing, which was significant, since he had always received top or co-starring billing from the time of *Captain Blood*.

The Sun Also Rises was also the most expensive film (although it didn't look it) in which Flynn appeared, costing a reputed $5 million. It was photographed in Pamplona, Paris, Biarritz, and in Mexico in Morelia and Mexico City, with

With Eddie Albert, Ava Gardner, and Tyrone Power

With Eddie Albert, Tyrone Power,
and Mel Ferrer

the scenes at Pamplona and Morelia depicting the colorful bullfight fiesta being the most satisfying.

Hemingway's 1926 novel about a quintet of "lost generation" expatriates who drink steadily and talk endlessly, and who are running away from themselves, is a difficult property to translate to film. Brett (Gardner), a beautiful woman with nymphomaniacal tendencies, is engaged to marry Mike Campbell (Flynn), but she loves Jake (Power), an American newspaper correspondent who is impotent as a result of a wound received during the first World War.

Hemingway's spare and stylized prose lets the reader attach more meaning to the words than meets the eye, but this is not always playable in filmic terms. Also, the characters in the novel are young and disillusioned by World War I, whereas the principals in the film are much too old. The problems and emotional states of the lost generation had significance at the time of the book's publication, but for audiences of 1957 there was little or no identification or frame of reference.

However, Flynn stole the show and turned in a fine performance—if performance is the word; perhaps reflection of his disintegrated self would be more proper. He received excellent notices with many references to a successful comeback.

The faded actor was able to capture the world-weariness, the charming façade, the quick to temper, the mean drunk, the roistering hedonist, the buffoon, and finally the tragic, lonely figure—sitting on the edge of a bed. He seemed to be contemplating the waste, the emotional bankruptcy, and the essential hollowness of his life. Flynn knew the colorings and complexities of a Mike Campbell only too well.

With Eddie Albert and
Tyrone Power

213

Too Much, Too Soon

1958 A Warner Brothers Picture. Directed by Art Napoleon. Produced by Henry Blanke. Screenplay by Art and Jo Napoleon. Based on the book by Diana Barrymore and Gerold Frank. Music by Ernest Gold. Directors of Photography: Nick Musuraca and Carl Guthrie. Dialogue Supervisor: Eugene Busch. Film Editor: Owen Marks. Art Director: John Beckman. Set Decorator: George James Hopkins. Costumes: Orry-Kelly. Make-up: Gordon Bau. Sound: Francis E. Stahl. Assistant Director: George Vieira. Running time: 121 minutes.

With Dorothy Malone

With John Dennis

CAST

Diana Barrymore	DOROTHY MALONE
John Barrymore	ERROL FLYNN
Vincent Bryant	Efrem ZIMBALIST, Jr.
John Howard	Ray Danton
Michael Strange	Neva Patterson
Charlie Snow	Murray Hamilton
Lincoln Forrester	Martin Milner
Walter Gerhardt	John Dennis
Robert Wilcox	Edward Kemmer
Gerold Frank	Robert Ellenstein
Miss Magruder	Kathleen Freeman
Crowley	John Doucette
Patterson	Michael Mark
Imperial Pictures	⎰ Francis DeSales
Executives	⎱ Jay Jostyn
Assistants	⎰ Herb Ellis
	⎱ Louis Quinn

Associate	Robert S. Carson
Bill	Paul Bryar
Harry	Sid Tomack

FLYNN's contract with Warners had been settled and terminated in early 1954, his last picture for that studio having been *The Master of Ballantrae.*

In 1957, Warners bought the rights to Diana Barrymore's frank confessional, *Too Much, Too Soon.* Jack L. Warner in his autobiography says:

> When we talked about casting the role of John Barrymore, who had literally boozed himself into the grave, I immediately thought of Errol. Frankly, I missed his gaiety and taunting

With Dorothy Malone and Murray Hamilton

laughter and the excitement he generated on the set, and I sent him a letter offering him the part. . . . He came back to the lot, but I could not bear to watch him struggle through take after take. The once strong and handsome face was puffy and gray, the dancing shimmer was gone from his eyes, and there was no longer a spring in his step. He was playing the part of a drunken actor, and he didn't need any method system to get him in the mood. He *was* drunk. *Too much too soon.* The words should have been carved on a tombstone at the time, for he was one of the living dead.

The sordid, depressing story of Diana Barrymore, John's daughter by his first wife, "Michael Strange" (real name: Blanche Oelrichs), was a cheap, incomplete—presumably because of legal clearances—screen treatment. Diana is represented as a child who sought love but was denied it by her busy parents. Her loneliness provides the reason for her frantic romances, marriages, and alcoholism.

Diana's first husband was actor Bramwell Fletcher. In the film he is fictionalized as "Vincent Bryant" (Zimbalist). Husband number two, John Howard, a tennis player (Danton), is shown as a vindictive sadist. He is replaced by the real-life actor Robert Wilcox (Kemmer), a reformed—but not for long—drunkard.

Flynn was a great admirer of Barrymore, becoming a crony and spending considerable time with him in the last years before the Great Profile's death in 1942. He often amused his friends with impressions of Barrymore. However, in discussing the role for the film, Flynn said: "To play Jack was hard. You don't give an imitation—that's bad. I tried to take him before he became the buffoon, before he started to burlesque himself. It was a period of his life when he was lost and trying to get hold of himself."

Because of an inadequate script, poor direction, and Flynn's condition, it is only a partially realized characterization with a few isolated moments of truth.

Barrymore and Flynn's saga had certain parallels, the primary one being their dedicated wish to destroy themselves. The difference was that it took Barrymore sixty-two years to accomplish this end and Flynn only fifty.

The Roots of Heaven

1958   A Darryl F. Zanuck Production. Released by 20th Century-Fox. CinemaScope; Color by DeLuxe. Directed by John Huston. Produced by Darryl F. Zanuck. Associate Producer: Robert Jacks. Screenplay by Romain Gary and Patrick Leigh-Fermor. Based on the novel by Romain Gary. Music by Malcolm Arnold. Minna's Theme by Henri Patterson. Director of Photography: Oswald Morris. Second Unit Photography: Skeets Kelly, Henri Persin, and Gilles Bonneau. Film Editor: Russell Lloyd. Art Director: Stephen Grimes. Associate Art Director: Raymond Gabutti. Set Decorator: Bruno Avesani. Costumes: Rosine Delamare. Make-up: George Frost. Sound: Basil Fenton Smith. Special Effects: Fred Etcheverry. Special Photographic Effects: L. B. Abbott. Assistant Director: Carlo Lastricati. Technical Adviser: Claude Hettier de Boislambert. Production Manager: Guy Luongo. Script Girl: Angela Allen. Running time: 125 minutes.

With Juliette Greco

217

With Juliette Greco

CAST		
Major Forsythe	ERROL FLYNN	
Minna	JULIETTE GRECO	
Morel	TREVOR HOWARD	
Abe Fields	EDDIE ALBERT	
Cy Sedgewick	ORSON WELLES	
Saint Denis	Paul LUKAS	
Orsini	Herbert LOM	
Habib	Gregoire Aslan	
Governor	Andre Luguet	
Peer Qvist	Friedrich Ledebur	
Waitari	Edric Connor	
The Baron	Olivier Hussenot	
Major Scholscher	Pierre Dudan	
De Vries	Marc Doelnitz	
Madjumba	Dan Jackson	
Haas	Maurice Cannon	

Cerisot	Jacques Marin
Korotoro	Habib Benglia
Yussef	Bachir Touré
A.D.C.	Alain Saury
N'Dolo	Roscoe Stallworth
Inguele	Assane Fall
Father Fargue	Francis de Wolff

FOR the third film in a row Flynn played a drunk: this time it was Major Forsythe, the British deserter who goes along with a group of adventurers, opportunists, and exploiters to aid the idealist, Morel (Howard), in his zealous effort to preserve the African elephants, "the last free thing on earth," and symbol of freedom, friendship, and dignity in Morel's lonely world.

With Juliette Greco

With Trevor Howard, Olivier Hussenot, Juliette Greco, and Eddie Albert

The title supposedly refers to an old Arabian proverb: "The Roots of Heaven are embedded deeply in the soul of man, but of the heavens themselves, man knows nothing but the gripping roots."

Both Darryl Zanuck and John Huston became interested in the Romain Gary novel, and decided to do it together. Unfortunately, the saga of their expedition into French Equatorial Africa with a full cast and crew is much more interesting and exciting than the resulting film. Temperatures were 140° by day and 90° by night; malaria, amoebic dysentery, and other tropical diseases took an enormous toll on the party. Eddie Albert collapsed from sunstroke and was actually delirious for a few days. Flynn fortified himself with vodka and juices, managing to avoid any physical disabilities until the company returned to Paris for interior photography, whereupon he was hit with a recurrence of his old enemy, malaria.

Originally, William Holden was to play the role of Morel with Flynn in support, but due to some contractual problems between Holden and Paramount, Holden had to be replaced by Trevor Howard, with Flynn then assuming top billing.

Flynn's role in the film was changed, incidentally. In the book he was a brainwashed American officer who had broadcast for the Communists in Korea. In the film he is a British officer who betrayed his fellow officers to the Nazis. Flynn's by now familiar variations on a sot were adequate, but he had little to do.

Aside from the fact that the film did not come off in general, it could just have easily been shot on a back lot, so mundane is the location coverage. Even John Huston has been quoted as saying, "The pictures that turn out to be the most difficult to make, usually turn out to be the worst—like *Roots of Heaven*."

The script called for Flynn to die a hero's death—his ninth and last screen death. His own was only a year away.

Cuban Rebel Girls

1959   An Exploit Films Production. Released by Joseph Brenner Associates. Produced and Directed by Barry Mahon. Written and Narrated by Errol Flynn. Running time: 68 minutes.

CAST   *Himself*   ERROL FLYNN
       Beverly   Beverly AADLAND
       Johnny   John MacKAY
       Jacqueline   Jackie Jackler
       Maria   Marie Edmund
                Ben Ostrovsky
                Regnier Sanchez
                Esther Oliva
                Todd Brody
                Al Brown
                Clelle Mahon

IT would be well to consider *The Roots of Heaven* as the last Flynn film, but there was one other—a miserable screen epitaph called *Cuban Rebel Girls*. This was a semidocumentary with a very weak story line, written and co-produced by Flynn as a tax write-off at a time when he was impressed with Castro.

Flynn is presented as being on assignment as a correspondent, coming to Cuba to interview Castro and write stories about his campaign. The disintegrated actor looked horrifyingly tired and aged. His current girl friend, sixteen-year-old Beverly Aadland, played the female lead, an American who loves one of the mercenaries helping Castro.

Skirmishes in the Sierra Maestra Mountains, the burning of sugar-cane fields, and a raid on a

*With John MacKay and
Jackie Jackler*

sugar mill are the principal action, but they are handled in neither a convincing nor melodramatic fashion.

Cheaply filmed and put together in Cuba and New York, some of the footage, and especially the sound, have an almost amateur quality. The film's political viewpoint is vague; Flynn pontificates about fighting for freedom and overthrowing despots. Truly a tragic last picture, a sad ending for the robust and heroic cavalier of a number of screen classics.

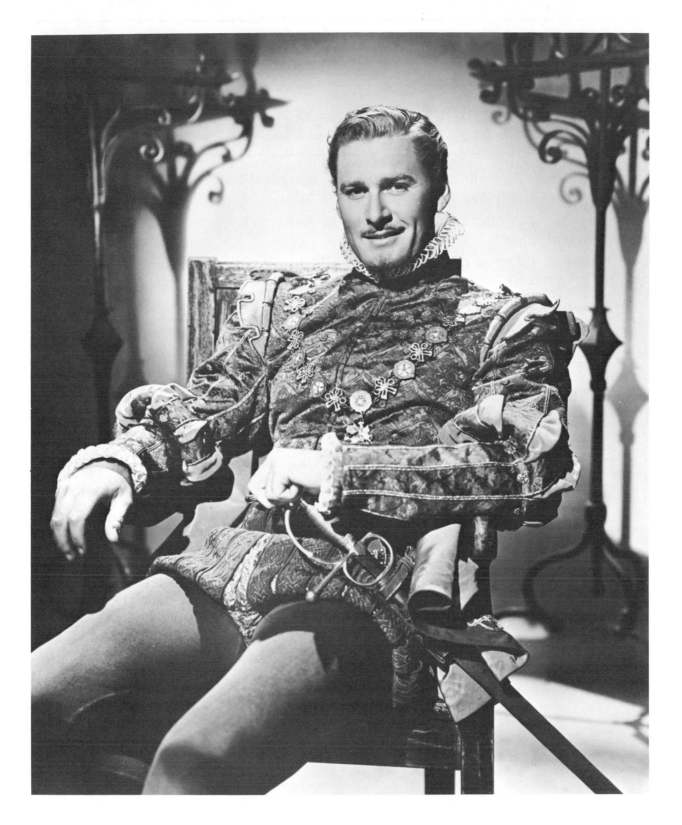